This Book belongs to the
Sparsholt College Library

RE CO   CULTURE.

KT-173-789

SPARSHOLT COLLEGE
13 MAR 1990
HAMPSHIRE

WITHDRAWN

PLEASE ENTER ON ISSUE SLIP:

AUTHOR   NICHOLAS   A.

TITLE   The Boston Terrier

ACCESSION NO.   9004244

THE RESOURCE CENTRE SPARSHOLT COLLEGE, HAMPSHIRE

ACCESSION No:

9004244

CLASS NUMBER: SAC 636.72 BOS

THE
BOSTON
TERRIER

BY ANNA KATHERINE NICHOLAS

Title page photo: Ch. El-Bo's Rudy Is A Dandy, the winner of 18 Best in Show awards, is a homebred owned by Eleanor and Bob Candland, Lake Elsinore, California. Considered by many authorities to be the finest of the breed they have seen, this little dog has had tremendous impact on the American Dog Fancy. He was No. 2 Non Sporting Dog in the nation, *Kennel Review System,* for 1981 (the first time achieved by a Boston Terrier since the system started), and he has at least eight Specialty Bests in addition to the above-mentioned all-breed victories.

© **1988 by T.F.H. Publications, Inc.**

Distributed in the UNITED STATES by T.F.H. Publications, Inc., One T.F.H. Plaza, Neptune City, NJ 07753; in CANADA to the Pet Trade by H & L Pet Supplies Inc., 27 Kingston Crescent, Kitchener, Ontario N2B 2T6; Rolf C. Hagen Ltd., 3225 Sartelon Street, Montreal 382 Quebec; in CANADA to the Book Trade by Macmillan of Canada (A Division of Canada Publishing Corporation), 164 Commander Boulevard, Agincourt, Ontario M1S 3C7; in ENGLAND by T.F.H. Publications Limited, Cliveden House/Priors Way/Bray, Maidenhead, Berkshire SL6 2HP, England; in AUSTRALIA AND THE SOUTH PACIFIC by T.F.H. (Australia) Pty. Ltd., Box 149, Brookvale 2100 N.S.W., Australia; in NEW ZEALAND by Ross Haines & Son, Ltd., 18 Monmouth Street, Grey Lynn, Auckland 2, New Zealand; in SINGAPORE AND MALAYSIA by MPH Distributors (S) Pte., Ltd., 601 Sims Drive, #03/07/21, Singapore 1438; in the PHILIPPINES by Bio-Research, 5 Lippay Street, San Lorenzo Village, Makati Rizal; in SOUTH AFRICA by Multipet Pty. Ltd., 30 Turners Avenue, Durban 4001. Published by T.F.H. Publications, Inc. Manufactured in the United States of America by T.F.H. Publications, Inc.

DEDICATION

To Alva Rosenberg, Vin Perry and Joe Faigel—three of our great All-Breed Judges whose careers in our fancy began with their love of Boston Terriers.

They will never be forgotten!

WITHDRAWN

Contents

About the Author

Since early childhood, Anna Katherine Nicholas has been involved with dogs. Her first pets were a Boston Terrier, an Airedale, and a German Shepherd Dog. Then, in 1925, came the first of the Pekingese, a gift from a friend who raised them. Now her home is shared with two Miniature Poodles and numerous Beagles.

Miss Nicholas is best known throughout the Dog Fancy as a writer and as a judge. Her first magazine article, published in *Dog News* magazine around 1930, was about Pekingese, and this was followed by a widely acclaimed breed column, "Peeking at the Pekingese," which appeared for at least two decades, originally in *Dogdom*, then, following the demise of that publication, in *Popular Dogs*. During the 1940s she was a Boxer columnist for *Pure-Bred Dogs/American Kennel Gazette* and for *Boxer Briefs*. More recently many of her articles, geared to interest fanciers of every breed, have appeared in *Popular Dogs, Pure-Bred Dogs/American Kennel Gazette, Show Dogs, Dog Fancy, The World of the Working Dog,* and for both the Canadian publications, *The Dog Fancier* and *Dogs in Canada*. Her *Dog World* column, "Here, There and Everywhere," was the Dog Writers' Association of America winner of the Best Series in a Dog Magazine Award for 1979. Another feature article of hers, "Faster Is Not Better," published in *Canine Chronicle*, received Honorable Mention on another occasion.

In 1970 Miss Nicholas won the Dog Writers' Association Award for the Best Technical Book of the Year with her *Nicholas Guide to Dog Judging*. In 1979 the revision of this book again won this award, the first time ever that a revision has been so honored by this organization. Other important dog writer awards which Miss Nicholas has gained over the years have been the Gaines "Fido" and the *Kennel Review* "Winkies," these both on two occasions and each in the Dog Writer of the Year category.

It was during the 1930s that Miss Nicholas's first book, *The Pekingese*, appeared in print, published by the Judy Publishing Company. This book, and its second edition, sold out quickly and is now a collector's item, as is *The Skye Terrier Book* which was published during the 1960s by the Skye Terrier Club of America.

During recent years, Miss Nicholas has been writing books consistently for T.F.H. These include *Successful Dog Show Exhibiting, The Book of the Rottweiler, The Book of the Poodle, The Book of the Labrador Retriever, The Book of the English Springer Spaniel, The Book of the Golden Retriever, The Book of the German Shepherd Dog, The Book of the Shetland Sheepdog, The Book of the Miniature Schnauzer, The World of Doberman Pinschers,* and *The World of Rottweilers.* Plus, in the newest T.F.H. series, *The Maltese, The Keeshond, The Chow Chow, The Poodle, The Boxer, The Beagle, The Basset Hound, The Dachshund* (the latter three co-authored with Marcia A. Foy), *The German Pointer, The Collie, The Weimaraner, The Great Dane, The Dalmatian,* and numerous other titles. In the KW series she has done *Rottweilers, Weimaraners,* and *Norwegian Elkhounds.* And she has written American chapters for two popular English books purchased and published in the United States by T.F.H., *The Staffordshire Bull Terrier* and *The Jack Russell Terrier.*

Miss Nicholas's association with T.F.H. began in the early 1970s when she co-authored for them five books with Joan Brearley. These are *The Wonderful World of Beagles and Beagling* (also honored by the Dog Writers Association), *This is the Bichon Frise, The Book of the Pekingese, The Book of the Boxer,* and *This is the Skye Terrier.*

Ch. Chamray Royale Trooper going from the classes to Best of Breed under the author at Lake Shore Kennel Club.

Since 1934 Miss Nicholas has been a popular dog show judge, officiating at prestigious events throughout the United States and Canada. She is presently approved for all Hounds, all Terriers, all Toys and all Non-Sporting; plus all Pointers, English and Gordon Setters, Vizslas, Weimaraners, and Wirehaired Pointing Griffons in the Sporting Group and Boxers and Dobermans in Working. In 1970 she became only the third woman ever to have judged Best in Show at the famous Westminster Kennel Club event at Madison Square Garden in New York City, where she has officiated as well on some sixteen other occasions over the years. She has also officiated at such events as Santa Barbara, Chicago International, Morris and Essex, Trenton, Westchester, etc., in the United States; the Sportsman's and the Metropolitan among numerous others in Canada; and Specialty shows in several dozen breeds in both countries. She has judged in almost every one of the United States and in four of the Canadian Provinces. Her dislike of air travel has caused her to refrain from acceptance of the constant invitations to officiate in other parts of the world.

Six champion Bostons owned by Ringway kennels, Denver; Champion Master King IV., Champion Kingway Cheerio, Champion Kingway Charlotte, Champion De Mar's Dream Girl, Champion Hoaholu Buddie Blink, Champion Kingway Journey Disturber.

Chapter 1

Origin and Early History of the Boston Terrier

The Boston Terrier is a very special little dog in the hearts of American dog fanciers — one of only several breeds to have actually been created in the United States from a British foundation provided by a cross between the Bulldog and the early white English Terrier. The combination provided what was known as the "bull and terrier;" from this background have come the modern Bull Terrier, the American Staffordshire Terrier, and the Staffordshire Bullterrier.

Back in the 1870's or thereabouts, products of the bull and terrier combination were enjoying considerable popularity in the mining districts of Great Britain, especially in the Liverpool area. Famous as ratters and fighting dogs, they were of remarkable intelligence and evidenced strongly the best features of both terriers and Bulldogs. Some of these medium sized brindle and white dogs were brought to Boston, Massachusetts, on ships from Liverpool, scoring an instant success with dog lovers in and around the Boston area.

So attracted were people to the new canine arrivals that they determined to breed them, their goal: to produce man's all-around dog.

Ch. Arroyo Anarchist, an early winner of Best of Breed in Boston, New York, Philadelphia, and several other cities, was owned by breed enthusiast of the early days Freeman Ford. This excellent portrait from a painting by the famed artist G. Muss-Arnolt.

The dog who caught the attention and imagination of the public during that period was Hooper's Judge, owned by William O'Brien of Boston from whom he was acquired by Robert C. Hooper. We have read that Judge was of unknown pedigree but favored the Bulldog more than the terrier in type: a dark brindle with white blaze and throat, cropped ears, a nearly level bite, and a screw tail, weighing about 30 pounds.

To this dog was bred a bitch, also of unknown pedigree, nearly completely white in color and stocky of build. She belonged to Edward Burnett, Southboro, Massachusetts, and her name was Gyp.

From this litter came a son, Wells's Eph, an evenly marked, low stationed dark brindle, white in face, weight about 28 pounds. To this dog was bred a bitch, Tobin's Kate, again of unknown pedigree, smaller in size weighing only about 20 pounds, a golden brindle with a short head as compared to the others. Barnard's Tom was among their progeny, whom history refers to as the first genuine Boston Terrier and the true founder of the breed.

Tom was smaller in size like his dam, weighing in around 22 pounds. Red brindle, he had a white blaze on one side of his face, white collar, chest and feet, and the characteristic screw tail.

A 20 pound, short-headed, evenly marked dark brindle bitch, Kelley's Nell, was bred to Tom. The puppies in that litter included one who became notable, Barnard's Mike, who, from what

A trio of famous Boston Terriers of the 1930's *(above, left)* Ch. Kingway Blink, *(above, right)* Ch. Captain Hagerty, and *(below, right)* Ch. Kingway Bill Boss. Three outstanding winners of their period owned by Mrs. W. E. Porter, Kingway Bostons, Denver, Colorado. Photos courtesy of Leonard L. Myers from his collection.

we have read, was the first to depict the true Boston Terrier type as we think of it now. A light brindle with white markings, Mike possessed the desirable full eye, an even bite, and short tail. He weighed in at 25 pounds.

The aforementioned dogs were the progenitors of the breed which became so popular as the Boston Terrier. Its principal source, so to speak. Others helped in the development of the breed, including other descendants of Hooper's Judge, but this was the main line of descent in the very beginning.

13

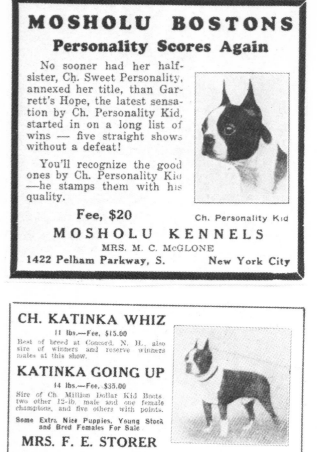

MOSHOLU BOSTONS
Personality Scores Again

No sooner had her half-sister, Ch. Sweet Personality, annexed her title, than Garrett's Hope, the latest sensation by Ch. Personality Kid, started in on a long list of wins — five straight shows without a defeat!

You'll recognize the good ones by Ch. Personality Kid —he stamps them with his quality.

Fee, $20

Ch. Personality Kid

MOSHOLU KENNELS
MRS. M. C. McGLONE
1422 Pelham Parkway, S.   New York City

CH. KATINKA WHIZ
11 lbs.—Fee, $15.00

Best of breed at Concord, N. H., also sire of winners and reserve winners males at this show.

KATINKA GOING UP
14 lbs.—Fee, $35.00

Sire of Ch. Million Dollar Kid Boots two other 12-lb. male and one female champions, and five others with points.

Some Extra Nice Puppies, Young Stock and Bred Females For Sale

MRS. F. E. STORER
42 Oakland St., Melrose, Mass.   Weight, 14 lbs.   Fee, $35.00

THE CHAMPION OF CHAMPIONS

"CHAMPION CARRY ON"

Needs no introduction. One of America's leading sires. Sired four champions and many other winners. GET BACK OF THE CARRY ON STRAIN THAT HAS MADE GOOD. You will, Mr. Breeder, eventually recognize the fact that you need CARRY ON blood. Why? Because he inherits in his pedigree the greatest producers the breed has ever known. That is why CARRY ON is "CARRYING ON." Build up your kennel—breed one of your females to him and be convinced. Stud. Pamphlet on Request

14½ lbs.—Fee, $25.00

MRS. A. L. BARRETT
3121 Sedgwick Ave.   Kingsbridge, New York City

Three very famous kennels of the 1930's. Advertisements reproduced from *Dogdom* magazine, for many years out of existence, which was in those days the principal advertising medium for the Boston Terrier fancy. Consequently, they represent some of the most prominent dogs, kennels, and breeders of the 1930's.

14

Chapter 2

Development of the Boston Terrier

Enthusiasm for these attractive brindle dogs was gaining strength, and their numbers increasing steadily as additional fanciers became aware of them, but limited principally to Boston and its immediate area. As the dogs became better known, so developed an ideal mental picture of what would be desirable in the breed. Gradually a rather miscellaneous assortment of brindle and white bull and terrier dogs began to level off and settle into the Boston Terrier type. Still in the 1870's and 1880's, several dogs appeared who made their mark and left a strong impression on future generations. A dog named Buster, owned by A.L. Googe, for years to come was found in the pedigree of outstanding Bostons. This dog had a son, Champion Monte, who sired many a winner and was called, several decades later, "one of the best the breed produced." His golden brindle grandson, Cracksman, was also a sire of champions.

Tony Boy, owned by F.G. Bixby, was especially notable as a sire of flashily marked progeny, having also been admired for his type. Sullivan's Punch we have seen described as a good dog, but unfortunate in that his markings were brindle, his main color white. Nonetheless he sired typical desired type. It was the crossing of

15

Left: This is an example of the 12-pound Boston Terrier, described in the original caption as "a perfect 12-pound Boston" owned by Edward Axtell. The dog's name, St. Botolph's Little King. *Right:* Ch. Pomeroy's Regards to Kid. Owned by Miss Emily Pomeroy, Dushore, Pennsylvania.

The famous Ch. Emperor's Ace, with whom Mary and Fred Lucas did much notable winning in the early 1940's, did much for his breed as a show dog and as a sire. Bred by Matthias Lynch, he was by Ch. Ace's Ace from Lynch's Transit Lady and was born in July 1940. He was a multiple Group and Specialty Show winner, gaining most of his victories in keenest Eastern competition, always owner-handled by Fred Lucas, Pelham Manor, New York.

these lines in breeding that soon was producing dogs of excellence.

As a precaution against becoming overly inbred, an occasional dog was imported from England when one of Hooper's Judge type could be located. Clearly those breeders were working towards a definite goal — not just another form of bull-and-terrier, but the **Boston Terrier.** Their progress was fast and sure.

The first dog show at Boston was held in 1878, with a respectable number of these dogs entered, although still under the designation "bull terriers."

In 1888, the efforts of the dedicated breeders was rewarded when the dog show at Boston provided a class for "round headed bull terriers, any color," the first step towards proper recognition of their carefully developed breed. John P. Barnard, Jr., a gentleman who was credited with great helpfulness and dedication to the breed, was the judge of this class. As a result of the chosen name for this classification, the breed became, for a short while, known as "the round head" or "Boston round head." Promptly a kennel was named Round Head Kennels (located at Providence, Rhode Island), showing their dogs successfully in the area around 1890. It was about this time, also, that the popular but unfortunate designation of "Boston bull" came into existence, used with equal abandon on both Boston terriers and brindle bull terriers.

During the final two decades of the 19th century the desired type became both known and recognizable. Then it was that the type really diverged sharply from that of the original bull and terrier progenitors as the efforts of the breeders bore fruit. The fact that this was a notable and admirable new breed was gaining acknowledgement and the Boston breeders were beginning to feel that this should be confirmed by official recognition of the American Kennel Club.

The American Bull Terrier Club was founded by these breeders in 1890, a small but active group proud of their achievement in having created this distinctive new breed. In 1891 formal application was made to the A.K.C. for recognition of their breed and their Club's membership in A.K.C. This was denied on the grounds that the breed was insufficiently well established, and that the new dog was not typical of a bull terrier. The breeders were in agreement with this and set about finding a new name. It is uncertain whether the name Boston Terrier was suggested by a friend or friends in the American Kennel Club, or whether the Boston club adopted a name that both distinguished the breed and named its historical background at the same time, but the choice was a happy one, and in 1893 the breed received official recognition as the Boston Terrier and the Boston Terrier Club was admitted to membership in the A.K.C.

At the turn of the century, Boston Terrier entries were growing in numbers at an amazing rate of speed. Early in the 1900's, it became quite usual for Bostons to provide the largest breed entry numerically at dog shows in the New York and Boston areas, and widely spread throughout the United States. More than 100 in competition became the usual for the breed, even ahead of Fox Terriers, Cockers, and St. Bernards which had been the previously established leaders. The high point came in 1918 with 164 of the Bostons entered in a single important show.

A new Standard for the Boston Terrier was written with care in 1900; then even more carefully it was revised and adopted in 1914.

Some of the more prominent early breeders of Boston Terriers, prior to 1920, deserve special mention in a book of this type. Among them are the following:

Dr. W.G. Kendall of Atlantic, Massachusetts, was among the foremost. Among his Bostons was Squanto II, sire of many champions. His kennel was established in 1877, and he was an important part of the breed's establishment.

Freeman Ford of Pasadena, California, owner of Champion Arroyo Anarchist, was a popular judge during the breed's early days, officiating not only in Boston, New York and Philadelphia but in other sections of the United States as well.

Other important "breed pioneers" from this period include Julius C. Feder, New York City; John A. Kelly, also from New York: Dr. George J.B. McCushing, Keene, New Hampshire; William F. Kubach, then of Elmhurst, Long Island: Edward Axtell; and Mrs. George E. Dresser.

When Vincent G. Perry passed away on February 22, 1985, it brought to an end of lifetime of Boston Terrier ownership, Vin having owned the breed since 1918.

The story of Vin and Evelyn Perry is a heartwarming one. The couple first met in 1919 when Vin went to purchase a Boston Terrier from Evelyn's mother, a lady who had been active in the

Left: Ch. Peter's Captain, a pre-1920 winner, owned by Mrs. George E. Dresser. An excellent Boston Terrier head of the day. *Right:* An early representative of the Hagertys, America's foremost name in the world of Boston Terriers over many decades. This is Ch. Hagerty's King owned by Mrs. George E. Dresser.

At the Brooklyn Boston Terrier Club Specialty Show in September 1938, Ch. Royal Kid Regards *(right)*, was the Best of Breed winner for Mrs. E. P. Anders of Linden, New Jersey. Royal Kid, *(left)* was the sire of the winner. Photo courtesy of Leonard L. Myers, Denver, Colorado.

This is the first Boston Terrier owned in the state of Michigan to complete her title. Champion Lady Luana.

Dr. W. G. Kendall was one of the breeders involved with the Boston Terrier breed during its early stages of development. This is his highly successful stud dog, Squanto II, sire of numerous champions and was, as his picture shows, himself a dog of merit.

From the early decades of the 20th century, Ch. Crystal Lady Sensation, the dam of champions, was one of many fine Boston Terriers owned over a lengthy period of time by William F. Kuback.

breed since 1912. And it was a "family joke" between them that while he never got the dog, he did get the daughter. A most completely happy marriage, both parties sharing a tremendous interest in the Boston Terriers, dog shows and dog people. They would have celebrated their 60th wedding anniversary in June 1985.

Vincent Perry started raising Boston Terriers in partnership with Evelyn's uncle, John C. Lunan, at London, Ontario, Canada, a partnership which lasted for many years. The Globe prefix was selected as identification for these dogs as Vin was then working for the "Globe" newspaper. After Mr. Lunan dissolved the partnership, the kennel became Globe Glowing.

One is not quite certain whether to classify Globe as a Canadian kennel or one from the United States, so closely were these dogs and these people associated with both countries even back then. A kennel advertisement from as long ago as 1922 reads that again that year "the dogs of this kennel won more winners points and ribbons than any other kennel of Boston Terriers in Canada. Wins made at the leading shows of Canada and the United States." Further along it notes that "The Globe stud force is composed of four of the most typical Boston Terriers ever brought together in one kennel in the history of the breed in this country (Canada) — dogs which by their performance in the ring and as sires have given us the right to make this broad statement. We keep only the male dogs listed below, and permit none of them to be overworked."

These dogs were Champion Globe Sweet William, who at that time was the only Boston in Canada, himself the son of a champion and the sire of champions. His progeny included Champion Globe League of Nations and Champion Globe Tiny Tim who were littermates. Tiny Tim was the smallest male to make the championship title in Canada for more than six years, and admired for the heads and muzzles he put on his puppies. Despite his small size, he was noted for litters numbering seven or eight puppies. League o'Nations was a very famous winner who defeated the cream of American show dogs as well as those in Canada.

Then there was an importation from the United States, selected principally on his ability to sire winners. A strong headed, beautifully marked dog, his extremely short muzzle bore not a trace of a wrinkle, something which breeders were still working on achieving in those days.

21

Vincent Perry was born in London, Ontario, Canada — and was a citizen of the United States. Prior to moving to the States in 1938, he had been a Director of the Canadian Kennel Club and both President and Secretary of the London Canine Association. For many years he bred and exhibited Boston Terriers in the Detroit area of Michigan, moving to California in later years.

Two of the Perrys' most famous Bostons through the years have been Champion Globe Glowing All By Himself and Champion Globe Glowing Perfection. These two sired in the area of 31 and 17 champions respectively. Glowing Perfection is in the Beaters Hall of Fame.

Many of the readers of this book will have enjoyed Vin Perry's writing in *Dog World*, *Kennel Review*, and his books *The Complete Boston Terrier* and *Skitch* (The Message of the Roses). Dog Journalist of the Year in 1970, 1971 and 1973, he was the first writer to earn permanent induction into the *Kennel Review Hall of Fame*. Also, he was awarded the "Fido" as Dog Writer of the Year in 1972. And in 1984, he was honored by the Senior Dog Judges Association of America for his years as a judge, during which he had become one of America's most deeply loved and highly respected all breed authorities.

One cannot help but ponder the truly great judges whose roots trace back to the Boston Terrier Fancy! Vin Perry, as we have just discussed. Alva Rosenberg, beloved to all who knew him and admired almost to the extent of adoration. Joe Faigel, highly esteemed and very popular — all three early breeders and exhibitors of Boston Terriers.

The die was cast for Alva Rosenberg's great career in dogs the day he lost his heart to a lovely Boston Terrier bitch, when, as an eight year old he had been taken by his mother, to Madison Square Garden to see the dog show — the only dog at Westminster that year, so far as he was concerned, and one which he yearned to own. She was for sale, but at the considerable price of $800.00, more than a boy of only eight years' age could possibly afford. Imagine what that 1890 price would be on the inflated ratio of to-day! Alva never forgot that dog, and as soon as it was feasible he established his Ravenroyd Boston Terriers which included such noted ones as Champion Ravenroyd Rock 'n' Rye. Alva was one of our earlier "all-rounder" (all breed) professional judges,

Left: Int. Ch. Globe Glowing Beauty, by Ch. Emperor's Ace ex Regards Tiny Beauty, a Best in Show and Group winner from the mid-20th century owned by Mr. and Mrs. Vincent G. Perry, Canoga Park, California. *Right:* A famous and dominant Boston Terrier from the 1920's, Ch. Rockabye Dempsey. It is interesting to note the gorgeous quality of this marvelous little dog as we realize that he was a product of more than half a century ago!

Eng. and Am. Ch. Chappie's Little Stardust, the sire of 21 champions, from the 1960's period was owned by Dr. K. Eileen Hite, Star Q Bostons, New York City.

This is Ch. Payson's Miss Patricia G. G., incomparable Boston Terrier bitch owned by Mr. and Mrs. Charles D. Cline of California, a famous winner, coast to coast, during the 1940's.

who during his lifetime gained so many Gaines Awards (Fidos) as Judge of the Year that, in order to give others a chance, a limit of four wins to one person was placed on the award for future wins. Alva had a very special affinity for the short faced breeds, himself owning Bostons and, in his later years, English Toy Spaniels. His greatest mentors as a boy learning about dog shows were Dr. and Mrs. E.H. Berendsohn who raised many famous Japanese Chins.

Joe Faigel is another who was beloved whom the Boston Terrier people could call one of their own. For years the Faigels owned, raised and showed quality Boston Terriers. All three of these

Int. Ch. Globe Glowing Perfection, by Ch. Hough's Ringside Perfection ex Mississippi Easter Cookie, sire of numerous champions. Himself a Best in Show winner with Group wins and placements. Owned by Mr. and Mrs. Vincent G. Perry, Canoga Park, California.

Dr. George J. B. McCushing's Play Boy, was descended from Ch. Dallen's Spider. Note the Boston Terrier head in one of its transition stages from that of the "bull and terrier" to the Boston Terrier of later generations.

judges were the closest of friends with respect and admiration for one another's accomplishments.

It would be impossible to speak individually of all the people who were involved, during the post-World War I period, with Boston Terriers! The breed enjoyed a steady supportive following with enough truly knowledgeable breeding kennels to keep quality and competition high.

Some of the famous names of that era were A. Droll and B. Rosenbloom of the Hagertys; Mrs. Madelaine C. McGlone of the Mosholus; Mr. and Mrs. W.C. Ely of Elyria Bostons; Ruth and Otto Dube; Harry Clasen; Mrs. Hilda Ridder (who I believe was the owner of Champion Rockabye Dempsey), who raised Bostons in her private house in the West 70's of New York City, where I recall visiting her and her dogs one afternoon during the 1930's. B.S. Stahl was a busy Boston breeder, as was Mrs. J.R. Kurtz (Green Bush) in Pennsylvania; Mrs. Lida Britt; H.W. Kenwell (Ken Top); Mrs. E.P. Andrews, and so very many more.

FURTHER DEVELOPMENT OF THE BOSTON TERRIER

By the mid-1940's some additional exciting Boston Terriers had appeared in competition, three of the most memorable having been Champion Mighty Sweet Regardless owned by Claude J. Fitzgerald, Champion Yankee Bombardier owned by Emily Shire, and Champion Emperor's Ace owned by Fred H. Lucas.

Mighty Sweet was from Michigan, a honey of a bitch who had the dog show world at her feet and on many an occasion took the Group honors over some of the very famous Poodles who were dominating the dog show scene. Mighty Sweet Regardless was born on September 22, 1943, by Champion Regardless ex Fascinating Personality, and was bred by Margaret F. Roberts. Many a heart has beaten faster as fanciers have watched Mighty Sweet go through her paces on the way to the winners circle. She did the breed inestimable good in the eyes of the general public, and made those of us who judge Bostons admiringly aware of her beauty.

Champion Fancy Bombardier owned by Emily Shire. By E. Hymarque ex Huguenot, he was born January 5, 1942, and bred by Eric J.C. Land. He was generally acknowledged to be a very correct Boston.

Champion Emperor's Ace, born July 5, 1940, belonged to Mary and Fred Lucas of Westchester County in New York, then later of Greenwich, Connecticut. He was a son of Champion Ace's Ace from Lynch's Transit Lady, and he too was a consistent breed and Group winner in the hottest of competition who enjoyed a long and successful career. Mary and Fred Lucas were very active Boston Terrier fanciers as breeders, as professional handlers, and in the Specialty Clubs — people who contributed tremendously to the progress of Boston Terriers here in the East.

Albert Rosenbloom, from the family who had been known throughout Boston Terrier history as one half of the Droll and Rosenbloom partnership so influential through the Hagerty strain, seemed for awhile to be going to carry on the banner. But after a few years of highly successful handling, he decided he did not care to continue, so switched to another career. Those of us who knew Albert miss him sincerely in the Fancy. Two of the Bostons I remember with particular admiration were Champion Fritzie's Regards of Pequa, who was bred by Myrtle Young whose Pequa Bostons were among the best in the East during the 1940-1950 period, and owned by the famous theatrical agent Joe Glaser who wanted always to have an outstanding Boston and did—and a stunning little dog who did much important winning.

Anne and Bob Griffing were involved in the Boston Terrier world from the 1940's into the 1950's, and then became more active with Lhasa Apsos. A Boston of theirs who had significant impact on the future of the breed was Champion Griffing's Little Chappie, by Champion Hayes Diplomat ex Griffing's Miracle Madcap, whom they bred and eventually sold to Signe A. Carlson in Denver, Colorado.

Left: Vincent Perry at a dog show; under his arm, Ch. Globe Glowing All By Himself, by Int. Ch. Globe Glowing Perfection ex Torner's Sparklette. Owned by Mr. and Mrs. Vincent G. Perry, Canoga Park, California. *Right:* John A. Middleton of Cleveland, Ohio, with four of his Boston Terriers in the mid 1940's. The breeder of eight champions, including such dogs as Ch. Dan Hagerty, Ch. R. Wee Joy, Ch. Hagerty Wee Pride, Ch. Hagerty Wee Ideal, Ch. Our Wee Sammy, Ch. Hagerty's Wee Toney, Ch. Our Wee Dean, Ch. Ideal Queen, and Ch. Cherokee Wee Ideal.

Left: Ch. Showbiz Mr. Chips Regardless winning under judge Byron Munson (Byron's Bostons) at San Fernando K.C. en route to the title. Handled by co-owner Lillian Huddleston for herself and Arthur Huddleston, Showbiz Bostons, Northridge, California. *Right:* Finley's Little Chappie, owner-handled by Mrs. Myrtle Young of the noted Pequa Bostons, taking Best of Breed at the Boston Terrier Club of New Jersey Specialty in March 1961.

KINGWAY BOSTONS, Reg.
DENVER, COLORADO

Ch. Captain Hagerty
Wgt., 16 lbs.   Fee, $20

Hagerty Again's Sonny
Wgt., 12 lbs.   Fee, $20

Kingway Rockabye
Captain
Wgt., 14 lbs.   Fee, $10

Little Tommy Hagerty
Wgt., 13 lbs.   Fee, $10

Ch. Captain Hagerty

B. F. LIBERTY, Manager

8018 E. Colfax Ave.   Phone: York 6633

Two other very famous Boston Terrier Kennels of the 1930's advertised in *Dogdom* magazine.

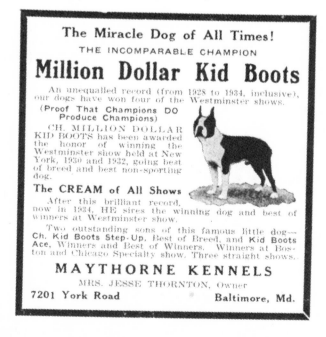

The Miracle Dog of All Times!
THE INCOMPARABLE CHAMPION
Million Dollar Kid Boots

An unequalled record (from 1928 to 1934, inclusive), our dogs have won four of the Westminster shows.

(Proof That Champions DO
Produce Champions)

CH. MILLION DOLLAR KID BOOTS has been awarded the honor of winning the Westminster show held at New York, 1930 and 1932, going best of breed and best non-sporting dog.

The CREAM of All Shows

After this brilliant record, now in 1934, HE sires the winning dog and best of winners at Westminster show.

Two outstanding sons of this famous little dog— Ch. Kid Boots Step-Up, Best of Breed, and Kid Boots Ace, Winners and Best of Winners. Winners at Boston and Chicago Specialty show. Three straight shows.

MAYTHORNE KENNELS
MRS. JESSE THORNTON, Owner

7201 York Road   Baltimore, Md.

28

Int. Ch. Mighty Sweet Regardless. Owned by Mr. and Mrs. Claude Fitzgerald, Wyandotte, Michigan.

Champion Griffing's Little Chappie was truly a power for good in the breed. He sired a total of 19 champions of which five were Best in Show winners at all-breed events. These were Champion Chappie's Little Man, Champion Silver's Fancy Chap, Champion The Black Eyes Imp, Champion Chappie's Regards, and Champion Chappie's Defender.

Some of these dogs sired by Little Chappie, and a goodly number of his other sons and daughters, topped the Non-Sporting Group and made impressive wins at important Specialty events. He was purchased from the Griffings by Signe Carlson at the New York Specialty when ten months old. Under Miss Carlson's expert handling he won five Groups and was judged Best in Show at an important all-breed event under Mrs. Beatrice Godsol.

A lady who played a major role in Eastern Boston Terrier activities over a period of time was Dr. K. Eileen Hite, whose dogs included a Westminster Group winner. This late fancier was a keen Boston Terrier enthusiast who gave an enormous amount of time and support to the breed. Her Bostons included American and Canadian Champion Chappie's Little Stardust, the sire of 21 champions, and two of his homebred sons, Champion Star Q's Brass Buttons and Champion Star Q's Pease Knutu.

NON SPORTING
GROUP
ANTELOPE VALLEY
KENNEL CLUB

Ch. El-Bo's Rudy Is A Dandy taking a Non-Sporting Group at Antelope Valley under one of his great admirers, Vin Perry. Handled by Bob Candland, co-breeder with Eleanor Candland, Lake Elsinore, California.

Chapter 3

Stories of Some Kennels in U.S.A.

ALEXANDER BOSTONS

Alexander Boston Terriers were established by Linda and Jim Alexander of Waynesboro, Georgia, after they had been breeding and showing Scottish Terriers for a period of time, during which they had decided that they would like a short coated breed without grooming problems. Space being another consideration, they wanted a small dog which would be easy to house, fitting nicely into the concept of "backyard breeder." Involved in Veterinary Medicine, the Alexanders had many opportunities to see and observe all types of dogs. The Boston Terriers appealed to them for their nice sunny dispositions, outgoing friendliness, and intelligence. In addition they had the requisites of correct size and short coat.

With all this in mind, the next step was observing the Bostons at the dog shows in their area, after which they were more certain than ever that this was the breed they would like to own. Then the search began for a good foundation bitch, and the Alexanders are quick to say, "We credit our good beginning to a beautiful red brindle bitch, Champion Country Kim Pic-A-Dillie," which they purchased from Janet and Warren Uberroth of Staten Island, New York.

Pic-A-Dillie was purchased in June 1973, giving the Alexanders a great start by producing quality Bostons and becoming the dam of four champions. Their own line of Alexander Bostons was started with the breeding of Dillie to two outstanding studs. These were Champion Tops Again Duke of Regards and Champion Good Time Charlie T. Brown.

Three of the Alexanders' Boston bitches have made the Top Ten: Champion Alexander's Ragtime Rosey, Champion Alexander's Magic Wanda, and Champion Alexander's Country Sunshine.

In 1984, Alexander's Polka Dot was Brood Bitch of the Year by producing three champions for that year, at the same time bringing her total to five.

During the years in which they have been breeding Bostons, the Alexanders have produced 21 champions who are carrying the Alexander prefix.

BLAZERMIN'S BOSTONS

Blazermin's Boston Terriers have become known nationwide for quality, soundness and beauty. This did not come about accidentally, but as the result of the dedication to the breed of Lt. Colonel Jim Cronen and his wife Patricia of Louisville, Kentucky, who have owned at least one Boston Terrier ever since their marriage in 1948. Patricia's mother was a long time breeder of Bostons, so it seemed only natural for the American Gentleman to become a part of her daughter's and son-in-law's household. In fact by now it has become a third generation interest, too, as Jim and Pat's two sons, James II and Thaddeus, are also exhibiting the breed along with their parents.

The name Blazermin was coined from that of the Cronens' Champions, Blazer of Top's Again and Mindy Mite of Little Acres. These two were purchased as show foundation stock from Mrs. Jill Ritchey at Sunwoods Kennels. The selection proved to be highly successful, Jim having finished Blazer in just seven shows (which included a prestigious 5-point major) with Pat taking Mindy to her title the same year. The first offspring from Blazer and Mindy to finish was Champion Blazermin's Valentine, who gained title handled by James II.

Ch. Alexander's Ragtime Rosey, by Ch. Tops Again Duke of Regardless ex Ch. Country Kin Pic-A-Dillie, was the first Boston Terrier champion owned by Alexander's Bostons.

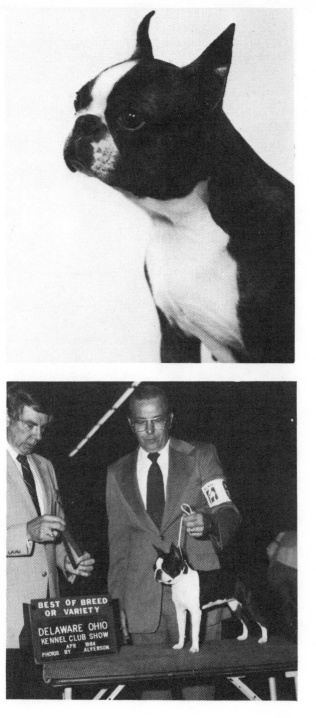

Ch. Blazermin's Family Tradition, by Ch. Zodiac Special Beau ex Ch. Sunwoods' Sweet Tradition, going Best of Breed at Delaware, Ohio, K.C. in April 1984.

BEST OF WINNERS

BLENNER HASSETT
KENNEL CLUB SHOW
JULY   1982
PHOTOS BY   ALVERSON

Ch. Blazermin's Mr. Mischievous winning under judge Michele Billings. Owner-handled by Jim Cronen.

The Cronens had also acquired a daughter of Blazer, Sunwoods Black Lace, from Jill Ritchey with the condition that she be bred to Jill's Champion Good Times Leroy T. Brown prior to shipping. This breeding turned out to be a super success, producing Champion Blazermin's Mr. Mischievous and Champion Blazermin's Waltzing Matilda. Both continue to produce champions, and offspring of theirs are owned in several areas of the country.

Although Jim and Pat had been breeding and exhibiting since 1960, they had not concentrated solely on Boston Terriers, having also been breeding-exhibiting Basenjis, Pekingese, Poodles, and numerous other breeds. This was not always easy; Jim had been a career army officer subject to constant re-assignments. While on overseas assignments, the late handler, then judge, Larry Krebs took over for them with their dogs.

Following retirement from the service, Jim and Pat decided that the sensible action to take in connection with their dogs would be to concentrate on the breed they most dearly love, the Boston Terrier. But it was not until they met and became close friends with the Ritcheys that they began to truly enjoy and succeed in the Fancy. Now Jim and Jill co-own several Bostons, all of whom Jim has shown to their titles, or is currently showing. One especially notable is that grand lady, Champion Sunwood's Sweet Tradition. She has been bred to Champion Zodiac's Special Beau (producing Champion Blazermin's Family Tradition); to Champion Mike Mar's Truly Special, producing Champion Sunwood's Classic Design; and to Champion Alexander's Dear John, producing Blazermin's Angel who is currently being shown.

In keeping with their ideas on planned breedings for type, temperament and personality, the Cronens utilize outside studs as often as it seems suitable to do so. Champion Blazermin's Family Tradition was bred to Champion Staley's El-Bo's Showman and produced Blazermin's April, currently being shown. Champion Blazermin's Valentine was bred to their own stud, Champion Sunwood's Sweet Reward, producing Blazermin's Taffy, also currently in competition, this one being handled by Jim II.

Since 1980, Blazermin's Bostons have finished 13 champions. Of these, eight were solely owned, three co-owned, and two breeder-handled. Currently the Cronens have three fully owned and one co-owned Boston in competition, and are specialing Champion Blazermin's Family Tradition.

BO-K BOSTONS

Karen and Bob Milham, owners of Bo-K Kennels at Phoenix, Arizona, were each raised with Boston Terriers and have had them continuously since their marriage in 1955. Although they have raised Bostons through all the years of their married life, it was only towards the mid-1970's that they started to exhibit their dogs. Since then they have produced and finished many champions.

The Bo-K line was originally established on descendants of the late Vincent Perry's famous Globe bloodlines combined with the Dahl Bostons belonging to Dorothy Dahl, these being the Bostons the Milhams chose on which to found their own breeding program. To date there are six beautiful champion bitches sharing the Milham household.

BONNIE BOSTONS

Bonnie Bostons are owned by Rita Otteson and Mae Wiger at Anaheim, California. These two ladies have been breeding on the Byron bloodlines since 1970, and take particular pride in being breeders-owners of the Best in Show winning brace which consists of Champion Bonnie's Rock-N-Roll and Champion Bonnie's Sugar N Spice, both by Champion Byron's T.N.T. ex Bonnie's Sweetheart O'Showbiz C.D.X.

ROBERT L. BREUM

Robert L. Breum, of Omaha, Nebraska, is the gentleman who had the honor of owning the great Champion Zodiac's Special Beau. This is probably not quite the way to say it, as actually I do believe that it was "Tony," as Special Beau was called, who owned Bob Breum. But anyway it is stated, I am certain that those who have themselves owned and loved a Boston Terrier will recognize the relationship being described.

Nobody loves Bostons more than does Bob Breum, who has had one constantly at his side ever since he was seven years old, except for the period of time he spent in the military service. To Bob, the Boston Terrier is the incomparable companion dog, and for

Bonnie's Bold and Brassy, daughter of Ch. Byron's T-N-T and Bonnie's Velvet Perfection, was born in June 1976. Bred by Bonnie Bostons owned by Rita Otteson and Mae Wiger.

Ch. Bo-K's Hey Good Lookin, by Mex and Am. Ch. Balboa Handsome Model ex Ch. Bo-K's Hey Look Me Over. Bred, owned,and shown by Bob and Karen Milham, Bo-K Kennels.

Ch. Bar None's Classic, bred by Robert L. Breum and G. R. Decker, Omaha, Nebraska, taking Best Puppy at the Boston Terrier Club of Maryland Specialty 1984. Bob Breum, who enjoys showing puppies and has finished most of his from the puppy class, says of this one "I think the loveliest puppy I have ever bred." The judge is Leonard Myers.

BOSTON TERRIER CLUB OF MARYLAND
BEST PUPPY
T&S PHOTOS   APRIL 14, 1984

many, many years one of his greatest pleasures has been in the showing of a beautiful Boston.

Bob is not a breeder at heart. In fact for as long as Kathryn Schuett of Bar None Bostons, was breeding, he never did any breeding but instead purchased his dogs from her. When Kathryn retired, he felt himself rather pushed into breeding as he felt that he could produce better than he could buy. Working ten hours daily at his job, and with various other responsibilities, he does not enjoy breeding. When a litter is born at his home, it is purely because he feels the need of new Bostons to show and own. All of the Breum Bostons live in Bob's home, never a kennel, and one or two go to work with him each day on a rotating basis. What better way to bring this breed to their greatest fulfillment in personality and intelligence?

Champion Zodiac's Special Beau was bred by Juanita Camp, born on December 23, 1978. He was sired by Champion Unique's Special Beau (Champion Beau Kay's Dusty Tops-Unique's Royalty Command) ex Champion Unique's Star of Zodiac (Champion Unique's Royalty's Kid ex Vogel's Velvet Cover Girl). Interestingly, one of his great grandsires, Champion Victor of Bar None; and a great-great granddam, Champion Christina of Bar None, were owned by Mr. Breum.

Tony's death at only five years of age, on August 24, 1985, was a tragedy to the entire Boston Fancy; and an unforgettble sorrow to Bob Breum who loved him so deeply. During his lifetime this amazing little Boston, owner-handled all the way, had won 10 All-Breed Bests in Show; Best of Breed at nine Boston Terrier Specialties; and 38 Group Firsts.

But despite his tremendous show record, his greatest contribution was as a sire; 38 champions by him have finished to date, with many others certain to follow. Not just carefully finished champions, but Bostons of quality and excellence who have also done notable winning throughout the United States and are themselves producing progeny of merit.

Champion Zodiac's Special Beau was Stud Dog of the Year for at least three consecutive years. Posthumously he was named Sire of the Year by the Western Boston Terrier Club of Chicago and the Boston Terrier Club of America.

Special Beau ("Tony") died of a pain killer administered to help him overcome the effects of an eye injury—one of the tragedies of the Boston Terrier world!

Tributes to this dog have come from far and near.

Bob Breum is a person who really enjoys handling his Bostons. He never shows a dog unless he has faith in it, and he honestly believes it has something to offer. As he says, "He may not be perfect, but he's a beautiful specimen." His particular pleasure is in showing puppies, and in campaigning a special, plus, of course, the deep interest he has taken over the years in obedience.

Since he has never been that much of a breeder, Bob did not, so far as we know, take for himself a kennel name, but seems to have adopted Bar None since the retirement of the original owner, Kathryn Schuett.

BYRON'S BOSTONS

Byron's Boston Terriers are legendary in this breed, having produced and owned some of the very greatest. All the way back in 1919 Byron's Lady Jane was being handled by Gene Marchise for owner Byron Munson whose interest in the breed has never faltered over the many years since then.

In 1929 Byron and Doris Munson were married, he having had the good fortune to find a most attractive young lady who enthusiastically shared his love of Boston Terriers. Also during this same year he had the fun of piloting his own class dog, Byron's Choux Choux, to a hotly contested Best of Breed win in an entry of 85 Boston Terriers at the prestigious Long Beach Kennel Club Dog Show.

Ever since then, the Munsons, who live in North Hollywood, California, have been gaining the respect of their fellow fanciers by campaigning truly outstanding quality Bostons to exciting show records. This has been accomplished despite the fact that their litters have been bred only on a limited basis, and that they have been shown only when one or both owners could be present to personally enjoy the occasion.

In 1949 a most gorgeous Boston bitch, Byron's Buttons N' Bows, made her appearance in the show ring. A daughter of Champion Hough's Ringside Perfection ex Model Kid's Sweetheart, her show career lasted exactly the length of time it took her to gain title. Frosting on the cake was that while doing so she col-

This is the famous Ch. Byron's Rise and Shine owned by Doris and Byron Munson. An outstanding winner of the 1960's. "Rover" had five All-Breed Bests in Show plus seven Specialties and dozens of Group wins and placements. An acknowledged stand-out in the Boston Terrier world.

lected first in four Non-Sporting Groups from the classes. She will also be remembered by the Fancy as the granddam of Champion Byron's Short-N-Sweet and Champion Byron's Rise and Shine.

American, Canadian, and Mexican Champion Byron's Short-N-Sweet, who had been born in 1955, handled by Harry Sangster established a record of 101 times Best of Breed, 68 Group placements of which 12 were firsts; and for three consecutive years was Top Winning Boston Terrier in the Nation, Phillips System.

Champion Byron's Rise -N- Shine, ("Rover" to his friends), had on his record five all-breed Bests in Show, seven Specialty Club Bests of Breed, 16 Group firsts, and 66 Group placements from 72 times Best of Breed. In 1966 he wound up seventh among the Top Ten Non-Sporting Dogs in the Country (Phillips System). Three times consecutively he was nominated for Best Western Non-Sporting Dog by *Kennel Review* magazine, the only Boston ever nominated for this honor. He won the Beaters Award for Top Non-Sporting Dog for 1967, then retired in December of the following year.

During 1963, the Munsons showed a beautiful little bitch known as Byron's Hide N' Seek. She is another to whom the title came easily, after which she went on to gain a Companion Dog Degree (C.D.) to the tremendous pleasure of her owners. She was a daughter of the Vincent Perrys' Champion Globe Glowing All By Himself from Lindgren's Pupsy.

Champion Byron's Ruff N' Ready, by Nip N' Tuck ex Killary's Becky Thatcher, was another Buttons grandson to go down in history. As a show dog, his achievements included 21 Bests of Breed, three Group firsts, and more than ten Group placements, earning No. 3 among Boston Terriers in 1955 under the Phillips System. It is generally agreed that this dog's outstanding contribution to his breed, however, was the siring of Champion Byron's Rise-N-Shine. The Munsons have never maintained an actual kennel facility, as each dog enjoys life as a household companion. Here is a fine example of the belief that limiting quantity does not necessarily involve limiting quality; and surely it does much to enhance the enjoyment of one's dogs.

In June 1985, Byron Munson was involved in a very serious automobile accident. Mae Wiger and Rita Otteson, who have been breeding with the Byron's stock since about 1970, with Mrs. Munson's permission, have kindly supplied us with the information from which to present this story to our readers.

CHAHARY

Chahary Kennels, specializing in Boston Terriers and Brussels Griffons are located at Rockford, Illinois, where they belong to Mrs. Ira Smoluchowski, whose interest in dogs started under the Star of the Southern Cross, in Sydney, Australia. There it was that Mrs. Smoluchowski first learned the joys and the challenge of breeding dogs. In those days she had started with Pekingese, and then Boxers. Since coming to the United States in 1963, she has changed to different breeds, although she did bring with her one Boxer who lived to be 13 1/2 years old, and one black Pekingese male who, when he died in Chicago had reached the formidable age of 17 1/2 years. Her reasons for changing were that she did not have sufficient room in which to raise Boxers; and the climate for the Pekingese during wet weather was a problem.

Mrs. Smoluchowski has never liked to have her dogs confined to cages, but prefers for them to be able to roam and have freedom. After purchasing an apartment house in Chicago, it was impossible to give enough space to big sized dogs; and the short legs and long coats of the Pekes were bringing in from the outside more than she could manage by way of wet and mud during bad weather.

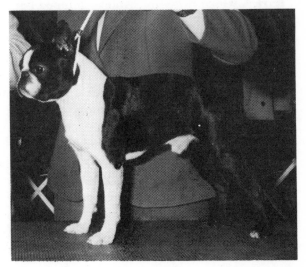

Ch. Chahary Mon Triomph Karmazin, by Ch. ML's Ace High ex Ch. Chahary Angel of Jovan, was bred by Helen Skibbe and owner-handled by Ira Smoluchowski. One of three champions already finished from Angel's litter of four males.

Am. and Can. Ch. Chahary Adonis Jovan, by Ch. Unique's Royalty Kid ex Ch. Chahary Beau-K Lalka Karima, gained his American title at only nine months old, and his Canadian title in just three showings. Jovan was a Specialty winner (including Best of Breed at the Cincinnati event in 182 entries of which 33 were specials) and for two years was in the Top Ten listing.

What was more natural than that she should turn to the Boston Terrier, which in conformation reminded her somewhat of a Boxer in miniature?

Her foundation in the breed was a nice bitch, Champion Chahary Balala, who combined the bloodlines of Command, to which she added Beau Kay. She has to her credit six generations of Boston Terriers, including many well-known and outstanding champions, as our readers will note among the illustrations in this book.

In the mid-1970's, Mrs. Smoluchowski, who had never quite gotten over her love of Pekingese, started to breed Brussels Griffons, which remind her in many ways of that breed but are higher stationed, making them easier for her to manage during bad weather — after which she also added Pugs.

All of the Chahary dogs are a delight to their owner, bringing her great joy. Also, they have changed her life in many ways, including the fact that she and her family sold the apartment house in Chicago and bought a house, instead, in Lombard, Illinois. Now she has a kennel on three acres of land at Rockford, Illinois — for her own dogs only, no boarders. Many big winners have already been born here, and many more will continue to follow as this is indeed a very dedicated fancier.

CIA'S BOSTON TERRIERS

Cia's Boston Terriers are the result of a long-time dream on the part of their owner, Mrs. Anita Ciannilli, who lives at Syracuse, New York. Says this lady, "Boston Terriers have always been my heart's delight. However, it was not until the past five years (the early 1980's) that I have been able to indulge this yearning."

The Ciannillis' first show quality Boston was purchased from Mrs. Alberta Clasen. Actually, she was supposed to be a pet, but she was such a charmer that her new owner could not resist giving the shows a try with her. Full growth she went 9 1/2-10 pounds weight. She took off like a flash, gaining 11 points in almost no time at all. Then sad to say, she developed endocrine problems and died at the age of 25 months. Heartbroken, her owners sought solace as quickly as possible. They found that Mrs. Jill Ritchey had a lovely show prospect bitch who was four months old with which she would be willing to part. Born April 18, 1983, she was to become, for Anita Ciannilli, American and Canadian Champion Sunwoods Bit of Brandy.

Bit of Brandy is a daughter of Champion Schubo's Roam 'n Romancer ex Sunwoods Lady Charlotte. Her American Championship was gained in three months' time, her Canadian Championship in only two months. Three months after the latter event, in February 1985, she presented her owners with a litter of three promising and lovely puppies sired by Champion Alexander Star Reward owned by Mrs. Ritchey.

Two of the puppies, a bitch and a dog, have been kept at Cia's Kennels for show and breeding. Their debut was at the Triangle Specialty in New Jersey on exactly their six-month birthday. Cia's Brandy's Best Beau took his class and Cia's Brandy's Best Bett took Best Puppy Bitch. With this as a beginning, Cia hopes to take them to their championships and to make their mark in the Boston Terrier world. Both are currently being handled by Miss Marie Heffron.

Ch. Clasen's Miss America, by Ch. Toby Junior II ex Ch. Me Too Samantha, is a Best in Show Boston owned by the late Harry N. Clasen. Photo courtesy of Mrs. Clasen.

The famous Am. and Can. Ch. Mr. Fancy Boots, by Iowana's Fancy Boots Ace ex Clasen's Trixie, owned by Mr. and Mrs. Harry N. Clasen, then of Albany, New York.

CLASEN'S BOSTON TERRIERS

Harry N. Clasen is truly a legend in the Boston Terrier world who, from 1906 as "only a real young fellow" until his death in the late 1970's was involved with this breed. As a breeder, an owner, and a professional handler, Harry has, over the decades, shown some of history's greatest Bostons and made many of the breed's more spectacular wins with his own and clients' dogs. Harry Clasen had a true "eye" for the breed — the undefinable talent for knowing and recognizing quality; and, in his case, for producing it. I have judged Clasen Bostons myself since the 1940's, and can say in all honesty that I never saw Harry with a poor one.

Harry's widow is living in Mechanicsville, New York, and still owns and breeds Bostons. It is to her that we owe thanks for this story which she very kindly has written for us.

American and Canadian Champion Mr. Fancy Boots and Champion Clasen's Cover Girl are two of Harry's Bostons from the 1950's. Boots was by Iowana's Fancy Boots Ace ex Clasen's Trixie, and he sired many champions as well as making a splendid record at the shows. Champion Clasen's Cover Girl produced champions sired by Boots, which were Bostons of tremendous quality. It is interesting to note the magnificent type and quality of these dogs from several decades back. And, as you will note in the caption of her picture, Cover Girl was chosen by *Popular Dogs* magazine to illustrate "the kind you like to judge, the near perfect Boston" in a 1964 feature, "Rights and Wrongs in Boston Terriers" in that magazine, calling special attention to Cover Girl's "beautiful head, topline, body and markings."

A dog who has had considerable good influence on the modern Boston is Champion Toby Junior II, by Clasen's Mastar ex Bee Bee X, who died in 1982 at age 12 years. At the New York Specialty in 1972, this outstanding little dog went from the classes to Best of Breed, gaining a five point major on the day. He has won numerous Groups and placed in others to become a Top Ten Boston for 1973 and 1974. Mrs. Clasen comments here, in her notes, that, "Of course Harry handled professionally for others, and while Toby was entered in Specialty Shows and the Garden, he did not get there," the latter in deference to dogs Harry was handling for his clients.

Toby sired 21 champions, which in itself is certainly a notable achievement.

Champion Clasen's Toby's Profile and Champion Clasen's Mr. Chips were full brothers by Champion Toby Junior II ex Shani Wynter Brooke, bred by Harry Clasen.

Toby's Profile completed title in 1976, then only four years later died on the veterinarian's table, a heartbreak which Mrs. Clasen has never forgotten.

Mr. Chips finished with a five point major at the New York Specialty in 1976, and was never shown as a special due to Harry's death.

Champion Clasen's Miss America was still well and happy with Mrs. Clasen in November 1985. She is a daughter of Champion Toby Junior II from Champion Me Too Samantha.

We are happy to note that Mrs. Clasen continues to breed Bostons, and that last year she purchased from Mrs. Staley a beautiful male puppy whom she plans to show when she feels that he is ready to go. His bloodlines will linebreed correctly with those of the Clasen bitches, so there should be some more good homebreds in the future at this kennel. Iowana, Grant's, and other such lines have been used successfully in the past by the Clasens.

Harry Clasen used to say that it took him "ten years of showing before he got his first purple ribbon," which is typical of the earlier days in the Fancy, when we "made haste more slowly" than in our modern world. This is probably why our veteran "dog men" have so thorough a knowledge as they have, as more time then went into learning one's breed thoroughly from basics on forward. Well do I recall my own early conversations with Harry Clasen, who was very kind and encouraging to a then young Boston Terrier judge, back in the 1940's when I was starting with the breed. Much that he said to me about Bostons has stuck with me through the years, and I have always admired his vast knowledge of his breed.

COUNTRY KIN

Warren Uberroth of Staten Island, New York, owner of Country Kin Boston Terriers, has a long history "in" Boston Terriers, having started with the breed around the mid-1950's during which time he has bred, owned, handled, or been associated with some 50 champions. It is our misfortune that Mr. Uberroth has never

Ch. Country Kin Tony Award during a brief specials career handled by Doug Holloway became, during six weeks of showing, No. 8 Boston Terrier in the country for 1984. Bred by Carl E. Santaniello, Jr., Tony Award is a litter brother to the Rosen's noted bitch, Ch. Country Kin Carmelina. He is owned by Warren Uberroth.

been one to collect pictures; therefore many which he felt worthy of sharing were loaned or given to other fanciers through the years, either for their own enjoyment or for publication in earlier releases.

It is quite true, however, that there is nothing quite like a current "star" to provide interest and represent a kennel's accomplishments. Mr. Uberroth's Champion Country Kin Tony Award is the star of his kennel at this time. Tony had a whirlwind career as a puppy, starting out at eight months of age with Winners Dog at the Boston Terrier Club of Connecticut Specialty. In a period which continued for only six weeks, under Doug Holloway's handling, Tony became #8 Boston Terrier in the country for 1984, with Best of Breed at the Triangle Boston Terrier Club Specialty. He is full brother, repeat breeding, of Mrs. Rosen's top winning bitch, Champion Country Kin Carmelina. Their sire, Country Kin Pippin, is by Country Kin Minute Man (Champion Country Kin Minstrel Man-Champion Country Kin Spring Fancy) ex Champion Karadin Our Mariah (Champion Courtbarton Emeraldisle-Champion Karadin The Jezebel). Their dam, Santaniello's Peppermint Pat, by Champion Star Q's Pease Knutu (Champion Chappie's Little Stardust-Clasen's Magnificent Doll II). The breeder is Carl Santaniello, Jr.

The Uberroths' Country Kin line was established from a foundation combination of Iowana/Clasen background, and it has surely proven highly successful, with Country Kin a prefix seen frequently in numerous pedigrees of today's top winners.

Mr. Uberroth points out that they are especially proud of their accomplishments at Country Kin as they have rarely kept more than five Bostons at any one time, all of whom had house privileges. As a multi-group judge now, Mr. Uberroth plans to discontinue breeding and in the future will exhibit on only a very limited occasional scale.

EL-BO

El-Bo Boston Terriers are owned by Eleanor and Bob Candland, now recently moved to Lake Elsinore, California, who have been breeding since about 1970.

Their first Bostons were a pet male, followed a bit later by a show bitch, from Pat Errickson in San Diego, from whose bloodlines they achieved their first champion. The Candlands have never owned any breed except Boston Terriers, and in 1984 the family numbered six. Recently Bob has retired and now that he will have more free time, I feel sure that show and breeding plans are in the future!

Eleanor and Bob have, through careful breeding and based on their original foundation, created their own bloodline of Boston Terriers, the success of which speaks for itself when one looks at its most famous representative, the fabulous homebred record-making Champion El-Bo's Rudy Is A Dandy.

Dandy has met with phenomenal success in the show ring, and is proving an outstanding producer as well. He is a truly tremendously successful show dog. Between October 1980 and September 1984, this fabulous Boston has won close to 90 Group Firsts, 18 all-breed Bests in Show, and eight Specialty Show Bests of Breed to his credit under a wide variety of judges. He is probably one of the most loved and admired campaigners of recent years, judging from the acclaim accorded his career and his quality by knowledgeable members of the Fancy.

FRASER'S RIVER CITY BOSTONS

Fraser's River City Boston Terriers are owned by Lois Fraser and located at Sacramento, California.

Mrs. Fraser is the breeder-owner-handler of her Bostons, and takes tremendous pride in their achievements — particularly since she had been warned that it would be next to impossible to finish them with uncropped ears, which she not only has done but gained Group awards and Best of Breed wins as well.

Champion Fraser's Handsome Elegance is the first dog this breeder ever has had in the ring, and now, after a good show career, he is starting out in obedience, which is another "first" for his owner. He gained his first leg on his first try, with a score of 191 ½. A son of American and Mexican Champion Balboa's Handsome Model (Champion Dahl's Look of Elegance-Dahl's Special Elegance, going back to Iowana's Velvet Boots) from Fraser's Mitzi (going back on both sides to Champion Derdon's Good Time Charlie), this dog was born in May 1979.

Champion Fraser's Merry Minstrelman was born in August 1982, a son of Champion McGee's Jason of Sacto (grandson of Champion Iowana's Velvet Boots Kato, Champion Byrmor's Sweet As Canbe, Champion Burnett's Special Top Step, and

Ch. El-Bo's Rudy Is A Dandy with his family, breeders-owners-handlers Eleanor and Bob Candland.

Ch. Fraser's Handsome Elegance, by Balboa Handsome Model ex Fraser's Mitzi, is an owner-handled homebred owned by Lois Fraser, Fraser's River City Bostons.

Champion Burnett's Special Delovely) from Fraser's Elegant Tuf Teena (by Champion Ashbun Acres Boston Straggler ex Fraser's Mitzi).

Mrs. Fraser's Bostons are in the 15-20 pound class. Her breeding program places particular emphasis on temperament and sound body.

GOOD TIME

Good Time Boston Terriers, owned by Thomas L. Enwright at Winter Haven, Florida, started in the mid 1970's with the very lovely Champion B-B's Toya's Tanya, now deceased, as their foundation bitch. This outstanding bitch is to be found behind all of the Good Time Bostons, and was the dam of four champions. Bred by Mrs. Billie Neigenfind, Tanya was by Champion Toy Town B-B's Chip's Rebel Again ex Champion B-B's Dude's Toyota.

Champion Good Time Charlie T. Brown, the pride of this kennel, was the No. 1 Boston Terrier and No. 10 Non-Sporting Dog for 1976. A son of Champion Torchy's Good News of Sunglo out of M.E.D.'s Mikki's Sunny Model, he was purchased by Tom and Jackie Enwright at the age of eight weeks from his breeder, Mrs. Lucille J. Sheets of Hialeah, Florida.

A multiple Best in Show (all-breeds) and Specialty Best of Breed winner, Charlie is the sire of 17 champions, and the grandsire of a great many more including Mrs. Jill Ritchey's Champion Milady Deacon of Boston, a multiple Best in Show winner who was rated No. 1 Boston bitch for 1982-1983.

Milady Deacon's sire, Charlie T. Brown's son Champion Good Time Jody T. Brown, was homebred by the Enwrights from their Champion B-B's Toya's Tanya.

Another lovely bitch belonging to the Enwrights is Champion Good Times Tanya's Toy, who is from Toya's Tanya and sired by Champion Chahary Adonis Jovan. She, too, is a homebred.

IOWANA

Without question, Iowana is one of the most famous and respected strains of Boston Terriers to be found anywhere in the world. Owned by the late Mrs. Florence Dancer of Des Moines, Iowa, who passed away during 1984, Iowana has been helpful in

Ch. B-B's Toya's Tanya, deceased, was the foundation bitch for all the Good Time Bostons. Bred by Mrs. Billie Neigenfind. Owned by Thomas L. Enwright.

Ch. Iowana's Velvet Coquette, by Ch. Da Bo's Velvet Kayo ex Iowana's Bridgett Boots, was bred and owned by Mrs. David A. Dancer. Owner-handled to many an impressive victory, this lovely bitch topped the breed at several Specialty events, including Western Boston Terrier Club in 1964. Pictured here winning an all-breed Best in Show at Council Bluffs K.C. under Forrest Hall. Sadie Edmiston is presenting the trophy.

the establishment, over the years, of countless kennels and blood-lines. Mrs. Dancer was a dedicated breeder who always bred her excellent bitches to leading sires and was never satisfied with the results until she had produced some of the finest. Her loss to the Fancy is tremendous.

Among the Bostons who have helped to make Iowana a household word among Boston Terrier breeders one finds the exquisite bitch, Champion Iowana's Velvet Coquette, an all-breed Best in Show winner, Best of Breed at leading Specialties, and a Group winner who was one of the many "greats" sired by Champion Da Bo's Velvet Kato. The sons of Kato include, among others, such admirable dogs as Champion Iowana's Jet Non Stop, Champion Iowana's Velvet Boots Kato, and Champion Iowana's Velvet Jaime, the latter the little dog who, back in the 1960's, created considerable furor in Puerto Rico where he was owned by Guillermo E. Vidal and handled by Ben Burwell.

Iowana Bostons were noted especially for their classic heads, so beautifully chiseled and the essence of the correct head-piece for a Boston Terrier.

Mrs. Dancer has attained considerable admiration and a large following as a judge. Hardly to be wondered at when one considers the knowledge of this lady, her devotion to the breed, and her talent for appreciating the finer points of typical Boston Terriers.

JEFFORDS

Mrs. Walter M. Jeffords, III, of New York City and Andrews Bridge, Pennsylvania, has been interested in Boston Terriers since the early 1970's or even longer. Her first ones came from Harry Clasen's kennel, handled for her by Mr. Clasen. In 1969 she had a lovely bitch in competition, Champion Clasen's Elegant Lady, a daughter of Champion Apposyte Honey Moor ex Clasen's Debbie Doll. Then in 1971 we find her the owner of an English importation, Court Baron Night Patrol, imported by Edna Voyles who handled him for Mrs. Jeffords.

Shortly thereafter, Mrs. Jeffords and Mr. Michael Wolf started co-owning Pekingese together. Mr. Wolf found Mrs. Jeffords' liking for Boston Terriers to be contagious, and in no time at all Bostons started appearing, too, under this co-ownership. One of the first was Champion Moore's Happy Romeo of Flash, bred by Mrs.

Ralph C. Moore, by Champion Moore's Ringside Flash ex Moore's Susie Q Baby.

Then it was that Mrs. Jeffords started breeding Bostons in earnest, with results which included those two stunning Best in Show bitches, Champion Jeffords Abigail and Champion Jeffords Constance as well as many additional winners. Michael Wolf piloted Abigail and Constance to exciting heights in toughest show competition, and over a period of some years other outstanding Bostons also were bred and/or owned at this kennel.

When Mrs. Jeffords decided to concentrate entirely on her Pekingese, and Mr. Wolf again established a kennel of his own, most of the top Bostons went with him. He continues to breed and show Bostons, as we all are well aware, and has used his foundation stock from Mrs. Jeffords to notable advantage.

Many other breeders have also purchased foundation stock from Mrs. Jeffords and are doing outstandingly well. These include Mrs. Honore Rosen and various others as you will note in our kennel stories. Thus, Jeffords Bostons have taken their place as an important producing as well as show kennel of the breed.

KINGWAY

The romance between Leonard L. Myers of the Kingway Boston Terriers in Denver, Colorado, and this breed of dog began for Leonard at the age of five years when his grandmother gave him, as a birthday gift, a daughter of Champion High Time. Looking back, Mr. Myers now comments, she "probably could not have won a blue ribbon at any show; but she had that wonderful disposition and temperament that endears the Boston to us all."

The first litter bred by Mr. Myers arrived in 1935, since which time he has continued to breed Bostons on a small scale regularly except during World War II when he was a member of the Corps of Engineers in the Pacific. This gentleman credits his success in regard to the Boston largely to the early training which he received from Miss Signe A. Carlson and Mrs. W.E. Porter, original owners of Kingway Bostons, who took him under their respective wings and cultivated so carefully his interest in the breed.

At the end of World War II, Leonard Myers continued his education at the University of Colorado, at the same time pursuing his interest in the Boston Terrier. Attending shows whenever possible, it was his custom to seek out the prominent and successful

Ch. Beau Kay's Gay Chappie, an important Boston Terrier co-owned by Mrs. Walter M. Jeffords and Mr. Michael Wolf, was handled to many exciting Specialty and Group victories by Mr. Wolf

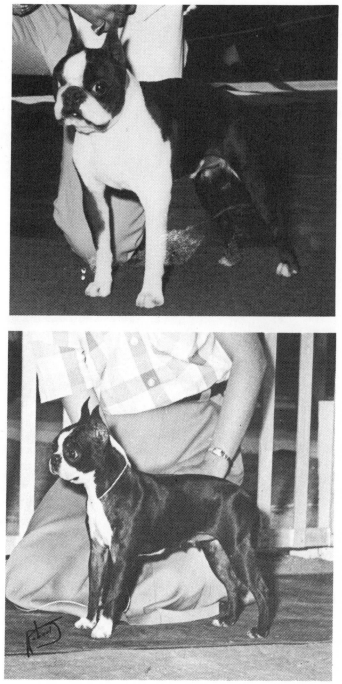

Ch. Silver Sonata, by Ch. Silver's Fancy Chap ex Silver Song. Bred and owned by Leonard L. Myers. Prior to adopting Kingway as his kennel prefix, Mr. Meyers' dogs had gone for a while under the Silver Dollar identification as noted in his kennel resumé. This pictured won in 1959.

Ch. Command's Fancy Salute, by Ch. Chappie's Salute ex Ch. Grant's Fancy Command. Bred, owned, handled by Leonard L. Myers. The judge is Alva Rosenberg who is awarding Salute first in a Non-Sporting Group.

breeders of the period, in order to discuss Boston Terriers in general and the breed's good and bad physical characteristics as seen in individual specimens.

His first big winner, although not his first champion, came in 1952 with the appearance on the scene of Champion Silver's Fancy Chap whom he had bred and trained. Fancy Chap went from the Bred-by Exhibitor Class to an all-breed Best in Show under the esteemed authority Vincent G. Perry, later continuing to win and place in many additional Groups as well as to win some exciting Specialties, including the Western Boston Terrier Club of Chicago. For a brief time after that, Mr. Myers operated a small kennel, Silver Dollar; but he soon learned that to bring out the best in temperament and showmanship of the breed, a Boston Terrier must be reared in a home environment. His very being is unsuited to kennel life, and he needs care, handling, attention and love. He also needs the opportunity to give that love and attention in return. So the Silver Dollar kennel was short-lived, and Mr. Myers returned to keeping only a few Bostons in his home.

He feels, quite correctly, that he is a successful breeder having finished many champions, the majority of whom were homebreds. A number of them have won Groups and place high in leading Specialty competition, but none were campaigned extensively and they were usually owner-handled. In Mr. Myers' opinion (to answer my question) the best Boston Terrier he ever produced was the exquisite bitch Champion Dynamic Doll, who won at the Parent Club and Western Specialties and was then sold to Ray Kibler of Maine. The author remembers her well and with admiration, having judged her on at least several occasions.

In 1971, Mr. Myers had the tragic experience of losing all of his breeding stock to a dreaded disease. It was a while before he was able to again look at a Boston, or attend a show lest he see one. But dedicated dog people do not stay away from their first love for long, and so eventually he returned to the fold to pursue his hobby with new and important bloodlines, principally Command, Iowana, and Unique. However, nothing ever could make up to him for the loss of his original bloodlines, 10 to 13 generations of them, which has been a real heartbreak.

For the past 25 years (since about 1960), Leonard Myers has been an American Kennel Club approved judge of Boston Terriers, and has officiated at many of their leading Specialty Shows from Boston to Miami to California and most points in between, some of them as often as four times. He has had his hands on some of the best over the years and, in the tradition of truly dedicated judges, each time has been thrilling to him. His interest in dogs has included English Bulldogs, Chow Chows, and Greyhounds which he has owned but never exhibited. He last judged the Boston Terrier Club of America Specialty in 1961, and will again be doing the National in 1986 in the San Francisco area.

The original Kingway Boston Terriers were owned by Mr. Myers's good friend Mrs. W.E. Porter at Denver. She is one of the two ladies whom Mr. Myers credits with having encouraged and taught him to appreciate and produce outstanding quality in Boston Terriers; and she was a pioneer in the breed, owning magnificent dogs of tremendous quality. Among the interesting clippings, photos, etc., which Mr. Myers had kindly shared with me are some from Denver's *The Rocky Mountain News* from back in 1934 carrying stories of the local Fancy at that time. In writing of Kingway Bostons, C.V. Cusack, whose by-line appears, says, "Denver is particularly fortunate in having within its city a kennel which ranks with the finest in the United States in the producing of some of the greatest show winners in the particular breed."

The article goes on to mention some of the leading winners there of the early 1930's. These included Champion Kingway Blink, one of the 16 homebred champions Mrs. Porter by then had bred; Champion Captain Hagerty, who at that time had never been defeated in show competition; and Champion Kingway Billy Rose, by Champion Mosholu Billy Rose from a daughter of Champion Mosholu Blink.

Mrs. Porter continued to breed and show outstanding Boston Terriers over a long period of time. How nice that Mr. Myers has chosen to carry on this name in his own Boston Terrier breeding of the present day. A very lovely memorial to this outstanding fancier who gave him the encouragement he needed as a newcomer when he was getting started with the breed.

LANBUR

Lanbur Bostons are owned by Jon Woodring and Wade S. Burns at Advance, North Carolina. Both owners began as breed-

Ch. Dynamic Kid, by Ch. Carry On Command ex Iowana's Velvet Belle II, pictured in 1968.

Ch. Chappie's Salute, sired by by Ch. Chappie's Mambo of Kingway. Leonard L. Myers, breeder-owner-handler.

Ch. Maestro's Kool Kid Miff, Group and Specialty winner, is owned by Jon Woodring and Wade S. Burns, Lanbur Bostons. Sired by Group winning Ch. Showman's Finale's Good News from Maestro's Saphire Blues (daughter of Ch. Zodiac's Special Beau), he is pictured going Best of Breed at Tidewater K.C., November 1985.

Ch. Maestro's Billy Whiz Bang winning the breed at Heart of America in 1985. Co-owned by Bob Breum and Julius Martell. One of the Top Ten Bostons in the Country, as of *Canine Chronicle,* October 1985. A multiple Group winner and a multiple Specialty Show winner, this outstanding dog was sired by the late Ch. Zodiac's Special Beau and bred by the Martells, Maestro Bostons.

ers of Shetland Sheepdogs and Beagles, in which breeds they have produced more than 50 champions to date.

Since they are professional handlers, Jon and Wade come into close contact with many other besides their own special breeds. And so it was that they became acquainted with the Boston Terrier through handling Champion Scott's Stuff N'Nonsense through her career as a special. In no time flat, these two fanciers had succumbed to the charms of the Boston Terrier, and promptly added some of these with which to start their own breeding program under the Lanbur prefix.

Their new "special star," over whom they are greatly excited is Champion Maestro's Kool Kid Miff, Group and Specialty winning son of Champion Showman's Finales Good News from a Champion Zodiac's Special Beau daughter. He is the backbone of the Boston kennel, with all of the Lanbur bitches being bred to him as foundation for the next generation of winners.

Lanbur Bostons currently house, in addition to Kool Kid Miff, five adult bitches and a young grandson of Champion Scott's Stuff N'Nonsense sired by Best in Show winner, Champion Staley's El-Bo Showman.

MAESTRO

Maestro Boston Terriers are at Topeka, Kansas, belonging to Willie Mae and Julius (Jay) Martell, and so named because Mr. Martell is a musician.

The Martells started showing around 1974 with a pet quality bitch. Luck evaded them in the beginning so far as getting a winner was concerned — until Susan Ruble and Shirley Livingston Canole were willing to sell them a lovely bitch, Royal Showmans Mona Lisa, who had already whelped two champions sired by Champion Candidates Roving Reporter. A repeat of this breeding provided the Martells with their foundation stock. Champion Maestro's Animato By Reporter, who completed title in 1980, was their first champion.

Since 1980, things have been buzzing right along for this couple and their Bostons. Six of the Bostons were sold to excellent show homes from where they have been exhibited to championship. An additional seven were finished by the Martells themselves by 1985.

The late Champion Zodiacs Special Beau, known as Tony to friends and admirers and owned by Bob Breum, (so widely admired by Boston Terrier authorities), was an important part of the Maestro success story. He and the Martells' foundation stock had many mutual ancestors, and so breeding their bitches to him brought the Martells some exciting results. They also fared well using Champion Showmans Finales Good News, again from pretty much the same background as the bitches the Martells were breeding.

As breeders, the Martells feel that temperament is of prime importance. Conformation and movement are next on their list, where they always hope to improve. Like most breeders, they try for perfect markings, but not at the expense of temperament, conformation, movement and showmanship.

It is a source of tremendous pride to the Martells that as of the October 30, 1985 issue of *The Canine Chronicle*, three Maestro Bostons are listed as being among the Top Ten for the breed in show competition. They are Champion Maestro's Sophie's Choice, owned by Mary Alice and Joseph Niebauer, Champion Maestro's Billy Whiz Bang, owned by Bob Breum and the Martells, and Champion Maestro's Kool Kid Miff, owned by Willie Mae and Jay Martell at the time of these statistics. Two others in that Top Ten list were descended from a male the Martells sold to Michael Wolf, whose Champion Albelarm Rather Special was bred by the Martells and is co-owned by Michael with Mrs. Alan Robson, for whom he is a highly successful winner. He is by Champion Zodiacs Special Beau ex Champion Maestro's Animato By Reporter.

The Martells have certainly achieved a tremendous amount of well deserved success in only a comparatively short period of time, with their dogs attaining high honors in many areas of the country where competition in the breed is at its keenest. They have now become a breeding establishment with which to reckon, although at the same time being a "home kennel" where all of the dogs are household members.

MIKE MAR

Mike Mar Boston Terriers are owned by Michael Wolf at Oxford, Pennsylvania, who has been tremendously successful not only in Boston Terriers but various other breeds which have interested him.

Mr. Wolf's first dog that I can recall was a lovely Italian Greyhound; from that time on he has owned, bred and/or handled Best

Ch. Moore's Happy Romeo of Flash winning Best of Breed at Westminster in 1973 handled by Michael Wolf. An important dog in the Jeffords and Mike Mar breeding programs.

in Show winning Maltese, Pekingese, Chow Chows, Pomeranians. He had outstanding dogs in several other breeds, too, in addition to his fabulous success in Boston Terriers.

Michael's active interest in Bostons got under way when he and Mrs. Walter Jeffords started co-owning Pekingese together which he handled. Mrs. Jeffords, even prior to her active interest in Pekingese, had loved and owned show Bostons; and so, quite naturally, Michael soon found himself involved with these little dogs, too. Then when Mrs. Jeffords decided to give up the Bostons, and Michael was opening a kennel of his own, upon learning that Mrs. Jeffords did not intend to continue breeding them, Michael acquired a number of her finest, including the fantastic Champion Jeffords Abigail and Champion Jeffords Constance, both of whom have gained rating recognition, are all-breed and Specialty Best in Show winners; both have contributed inestimably to Boston Terriers.

When Michael started owning dogs of several breeds with Mrs. Alan Robson, Albelarm Kennels, and handling them as co-owner, Mrs. Robson became interested in the Bostons and acquired co-

Ch. Fascinating Fancy Chief, 1966-1977, by Ch. Fascinating Fancy Ace ex Gimp's Delilah, was one of a litter of three excellent champions. Intensively linebred to Ch. Sovereign's Escort, The Little Dandy, and Ch. Fascinating Eddie H, he sired nine champions. Bred, owned, and handled by Joseph Niebauer.

ownership of Constance. Michael, with his keen eye, became aware of the quality to be found in the Maestro dogs and in Champion Zodiac's Special Beau, acquiring Champion Albelarm Rather Special from the Martells, a son of Beau. This dog, and Champion Albelarm's Special Too, have kept the Mike Mar and Albelarm banners high, both being in the Top Ten listings and whose show records during the first part of the 1980's have been impressive to say the least. Bred with Michael's outstanding bitch line, we can look for a great many additional winners from here in the future.

JOSEPH AND MARY ALICE NIEBAUER

The Niebauers, Joseph and Mary Alice, of Cassopolis, Michigan, have bred and shown 21 Boston Terriers to their championships, all owner-handled by Joseph. Their involvement with the Dog Fancy goes back to about 1950, or even a few years earlier.

Two of their important dogs over the years have been bred by Helen Johnson, Granger, Illinois. One was a son of Champion Fascinating Fancy Ace out of Glamour Girl's Model, and he completed his title at the Minneapolis Boston Terrier Club Specialty under judge Leonard Myers, owner-handled by Joseph Niebauer and owned by Mary Alice Niebauer.

Beau was sold by the Niebauers to Helen Fottrell in Ireland, where he proved to be one of the outstanding sires in the United Kingdom. A lovely son of his was later imported by Mrs. Walter Jeffords of New York, Champion Courtbarton Emerald Isle, who sired many good champions including several Best in Show bitches owned by Mrs. Jeffords and Michael Wolf, and one Best in Show bitch owned by Mrs. Ethel Braunstein.

Champion Fascinating Fancy Chief, 1966-1977, was sired by Champion Fascinating Fancy Ace out of Gimp's Delilah, and he was one of a litter consisting of three outstanding champions.

Chief was never campaigned extensively as a special, but was well recognized in the breed at his time. He was Best of Breed over outstanding specials at the Illini Boston Terrier Specialty (judge, Ethel Braunstein); Louisville Boston Terrier Specialty (judge, Marie Ferguson); and Hawkeye Boston Terrier Club (judge, Florence Dancer). He was always owner-handled and he was a homebred.

Chief was a product of intensive linebreeding back to Champion Sovereign's Escort, The Little Dandy, and Champion Fascinating Eddie R. Although used at stud only on a very limited basis, he sired nine champions and is in the pedigree of many an outstanding Boston today.

Champion Maestro's Sophie's Choice, born in April 1983, is the Niebauers' current "star." She loves to show, and finished prior to one year's age handled by Joseph Niebauer with five majors to her credit.

Sophie was purchased by Mary Alice from her breeder, Jay Martell, of Topeka, Kansas, at four months of age at the Hawkeye Boston Terrier Specialty. A daughter of the great Champion Zodiac's Special Beau, all-time top sire in the breed, she is out of Maestro's Sonata By Reported, and is the product of linebreeding back to Champion Royal Showman, Iowana, Tops Again, and Champion Grant's Royal Command.

Upon completion of her title, Sophie stayed home for a few months in which to mature. Jerry Rigden agreed to campaign her, and they have made a highly successful team as she has accumulated nine Group 1sts, seven Group 2nds, eight Group 3rds, and eight Group 4ths along with 56 times Best of Breed. They will continue showing for some months longer, after which Sophie will be bred. Needless to say, the Niebauers are looking forward to some exciting puppies from this great bitch.

PLEASURE

Pleasure Boston Terriers are owned by Ed and Cindy Galor at Lisle, Illinois. This is the home of the very famous and outstanding winning bitch, American and Canadian Champion Unique Pleasure Lacy, who is a homebred sired by Champion Unique's Royalty Kid ex American and Canadian Champion Rhett's Honest Pleasure.

As of November 1985, Lacy for five consecutive years has been on the Top Ten lists for Boston Terriers, All Systems. She has the distinction of 18 Specialty Best of Breed wins, which her owners believe to be a record for a Boston. Additionally she has been Best of Breed at 148 all-breed shows where she has gone on to 64 Group placements, these including 14 firsts, 14 seconds, 15 thirds, and 21 fourths.

Lacy finished her title in the United States at the Minnesota Boston Terrier Club Specialty on October 18, 1981, her Canadian title at Grey Bruce Kennel Club August 1981. Her prestigious wins include Best of Breed at the International Kennel Club of Chicago in 1983 (with a Group placement), 1984 and 1985. Her Specialty Bests of Breed were won at Minnesota Boston Terrier Club, April 1981, judge Ray Perso; Detroit Boston Terrier Club, November 1981, judge Ethel Braunstein; Minnesota Boston Terrier Club, April 1982, judge Michele Billings; Boston Terrier Club of Milwaukee, August 1982, judge Ed Klein; Detroit Boston Terrier Club, September 1982, judge Warren Ubberoth; Western Boston Terrier Club, June 1983, judge Leonard Myers; Louisville Kennel Club, March 1984, judge Emil Klinckhardt; and Detroit Boston Terrier Club, July 1984, judge Leonard Myers.

Lacy took time out to raise a litter in 1985, after which she returned to the show ring, handled by Stan Flowers, and has proceeded to do some of her strongest winning.

The Galors now are looking forward to the show career of Lacy's three-month-old daughter, which has just gotten off to a brilliant start with an all-breed Best Puppy in Match victory. May she follow in the paw prints of her dam.

FIRST IN GROUP

NON SPORTING

Am. and Can. Ch. Unique Pleasure Lacy, by Ch. Unique's Royalty Kid ex Am. and Can. Ch. Rhett's Honest Pleasure, bred and owned by Ed and Cindy Galor. This magnificent bitch for five consecutive years has been on the Top Ten lists for Bostons, All Systems, and in November 1985 her record stood at 148 Bests of Breed plus 64 Group placements. Handled by Stan Flowers pictured here winning a Group 1st under the author.

Regal Legacy Special Appeal, by Ch. Regal Appeal, by Ch. Regal Legacy Mass Appeal ex Rip's Penny Lane, starting out with a three-point major with Jose F. Negron handling for himself and Anthony A. Antolics, Regal Legacy Boston Terriers.

REGAL LEGACY

Regal Legacy Boston Terriers are owned by Anthony A. Antolics and Jose F. Negron and situated in Annandale, Virginia.

With a lifelong interest in the Boston Terrier, Anthony A. Antolics and Jose F. Negron founded Regal Legacy Bostons with the goal of creating their own strain within the breed. For this they utilized Chappie, Clasen, B-B, and Command bloodlines, instituting an intensive linebreeding program with some judicious inbreeding to set their desired breed characteristics.

Twelve homebred champions with nine more nearing completion of their titles in the last five years alone testify to the success of their efforts!

Foundation studs at Regal Legacy were American and Canadian Champion Simms Hihope Mr. Hobo, sire of 11 champions to date, and his grandsire, Neva Stewart's Champion Dude's Little Hobo, the sire of 19 champions.

Mr. Antolics and Mr. Negron are charter members of the Metropolitan Washington Boston Terrier Club, Inc., for whom they edit and publish *Capital Bostons on Parade,* an excellent monthly Boston breed publication.

Franklin van Der Spuy, South African Boston Terrier breeder, pictured with the two imports to his Springfield Kennels from Regal Legacy in the United States on the day of their arrival in that country. They are Ch. Regal Legacy Duchess Van Spuy *(left)* and Regal Legacy Rare Edition.

Bostons are a popular breed with South African fanciers, and have been exported from the United States to that country upon occasion.

One of the most successful of these has been Champion Regal Legacy Duchess Van Spuy, who went, along with Regal Legacy Rare Edition, as a puppy to the Springfield Boston Terriers, owned by Franklin and Adri von Der Spuy at Sasolburg, Republic of South Africa. These two were purchased from Regal Legacy Kennels, Annandale, Virginia, of which Jose F. Negron and Anthony A. Antolics are the owners.

Duchess has twice defeated the No. 1 Boston Terrier in the Republic of South Africa while still a class bitch, and it is felt that she and Rare Edition will do a splendid job there for the breed.

71

SCHUBO'S

Schubo's Boston Terriers are owned by Wes and Karen Schultz of Amarillo, Texas, who have been showing Boston Terriers in the Southwest area beginning in 1975. Since there were few shows held in that part of the country, the Schultzes had the opportunity to see the representatives of many top bloodlines in the country

Left: Ch. Schubo's Blazin' Star Gazer, by Ch. Georgia Girl's Chappie ex Ch. Schuba's Flashin' Go. Handled by Wes Schultz for himself and Karen Schultz, co-breeders-owners. *Right:* Ch. Schubo's Twistin' Dust Devil, by Ch. Georgia Girl's Chappie ex Ch. Schubo's Flashin' Gold Dust, winner of Group placements, bred and owned by Wes and Karen Schultz.

as they travelled to shows in Texas, Oklahoma, Kansas, Colorado, Louisiana and New Mexico.

The Schultz's first champion finished in 1976—Champion Schubo's Flashin' Gold Dust, bred by Ralph Vogel, who did so with three majors prior to her first birthday.

Champion Schubo's Travelin' Romancer, bred by Mr. and Mrs. C.J. Erwin, also completed title in that same year.

Champion Schubo's Inspirin' Candidate, bred by Pearl Ruble, finished in 1979.

Champion Schubo's Flashin' Gold Dust was bred to Champion Georgia Girl's Chappie, who was owned by Pat Errickson. From this litter the Schultzes finished their first two homebreds, Champion Schubo's Gleamin' Golden Girl and Champion Schubo's Blazin' Star Gazer, both completing titles in 1978.

Then, from a repeat breeding in 1980 Champion Schubo's Twistin' Dust Devil, bred by the Schultzes, was finished in 1980 while two littermates went to Dianne Lowes in Ontario, where, for her, they became Canadian Champion Schubo's Dashin' Dandy and Canadian Champion Schubo's Shimmerin' Nugget. Also from this same breeding came Champion Mi-Ki's Unique Royale Rocky, owned and finished by Marilyn Hirlinger. Rocky became the sire of Champion Rowdy Dowdy of Romance, bred by Rose Coulter and owned by Charles Schmidt, who was a Top Boston of 1983-84. Certainly, based on the above, Champion Schubo's Flashin' Gold Dust has proven herself to be a truly outstanding producer of quality Boston Terriers.

Other homebred champions from Schubo Kennels include Champion Schubo's Thunderin' Show Man, owned and finished by Rosemary and Grady Collum.

Champion Schubo's Mistin' Magic, owned by Lee Miller, is another to whom the Schultzes point with pride among the winners they have bred. Champion Schubo's Roamin' Romancer, finished in 1982 winning several Group placements along the way, including a Group 1st under the author from the Puppy Class. Romeo is now owned by Jill Ritchey.

Currently Schubo is being represented in the show ring by Champion Schubo's Streakin' Sky Rocket, born on July 4, 1982, out of Champion Schubo's Inspirin' Candidate by Champion Schubo's Roamin' Romancer.

The bloodlines behind Schubo Boston Terriers include Champion Royale Show Man, Champion Unique's Gay Beau, Champion Candidate's Roving Reporter, Champion Chappie's Little Stardust, Champion Patcha's Spectacular Star, and all of the excellent dogs represented by them.

BOSTON TERRIERS OF SCOTLAND YARD, LTD.

It was in 1974 that Mr. and Mrs. Marc R. Rosen, Rambling Ridge Farm, Park Ridge, New Jersey, purchased their first Boston Terrier from Harry Clasen, a little dog who became American and Canadian Champion Clasen's Campus Kid, who was just a puppy at the time he joined the Rosen family. Born in February 1974, he was sired by Champion Toby Junior II from Clasen's Sweet Tina, and he was the first Boston Terrier champion owned by the Rosens, having completed his title at the Boston Terrier Club of Miami, Florida, in January 1975 handled by Ellen Hoffman, when he took Winners Dog there. He was bred twice, but produced no champions.

In 1975, the Rosens added to their Boston family a fine young dog, Champion Jeffords Sherlock Holmes, a full brother to those famous bitches Champion Jeffords' Abigail and Martha, from Mrs. Walter M. Jeffords and Michael Wolf. Born July 30, 1975, he was by English and American Champion Courtbarton Emerald Isle from Champion Jeffords Bunny (who is also owned by the Rosens). Sherlock Holmes finished at the Boston Terrier Club of Connecticut in July 1976 by taking Winners Dog. He was used at stud on several occasions, and became the sire of Champion Scotland Yard Alfred Hitchcock.

Champion Jeffords Minute Man was born in December 1977, by Champion Beau Kay's Guy Chappie ex Champion Jefford's Martha (also now owned by the Rosens), and was given to the Rosens by Kay Jeffords. He finished in nine straight shows, despite being uncropped, and although he did not win a Specialty Show he left his mark on the breed with the production of his two handsome sons, Champion Jeffords Scotland Yard and Champion Country Kin Nicholas Nickleby, the latter bred and owned by Warren Uberroth.

In 1976, Marc and Honore Rosen purchased the outstanding young bitch American and Canadian Champion Dan Jee's I'm Suzi Too, bred by Dana Corum and Jean Colover. She had been

Ch. Jeffords Sherlock Holmes, by Ch. Courtbarton Emerald Isle (Ch. Fascinating Fancy Beau-Courtbarton Crown Jewel) ex Ch. Jeffords Bunny (Mrs. Jeffords Teddy-Jeffords Ladykins) is of the same breeding as that which produced Champions Jeffords Abigail, Constance, Martha, Ben Franklin, Andrew Jackson, and Storrs. Pictured in 1976 taking points towards his championship, handled by Honore Rosen to Winners at Elm City K.C.

born in January 1975, sired by Champion Toby Junior II ex Champion Clasen's Sweet Sue, who was, Mrs. Rosen notes, "according to records supported by the Clasens" the top rated Boston bitch of 1974, and who they also purchased.

The first weekend out, Suzi Too went Winners bitch at Providence in July 1976; also Best of Breed that same weekend at the Boston Terrier Club of Connecticut Specialty at Elm City, where later in the day she caught the eye of judge Dr. David Doane for a Group 3rd placement. It took her only ten shows in which to gain her championship, after which she was bred to Champion Jeffords Sherlock Holmes, producing Champion Scotland Yard Alfred Hitchcock, who was born in July 1977.

After this, Suzi Too started her career as a special. Exciting wins for her included Best of Breed at the Boston Terrier Club of Maryland, April 1980, over an entry of 100 Bostons. Six times she placed first in the Non-Sporting Group, with 22 additional Group placements.

Then came Champion Country Kin Carmelina, born in January 1979, bred by Carl E. Santaniello, Jr., sired by Country Kin Pippin ex Santaniello's Peppermint Pat. This stunning bitch was purchased by the Rosens from Warren Uberroth, whose kennel name she carries, having belonged to him prior to her present ownership.

Carmelina finished title in eight shows and was Best of Winners at both the Boston Terrier Club of America (1979) and the Boston Terrier Club of Maryland (1980). Specialed extensively, she won five Group 1sts, Best of Breed at the Boston Terrier Club of Connecticut twice (July 1981 and July 1985) and also at the Tri Angle Boston Terrier Club (1984). She was rated No. 5 Boston Terrier (No. 2 Bitch) for 1981; No. 7 for the rating year in 1982 and 1983 (No. 1 bitch, owner-handled), and No. 11 for 1984. In addition to her already mentioned five Group 1sts she has 38 other Group placements.

Champion Country Kin Scotland Yard Ace was born in July 1980, bred by Warren Uberroth, sired by Champion B.B.'s Dude's Little Hobo ex Country Kin Auntie Mame, now also owned by the Rosens. Ace finished at 11 months, and was Best Puppy in Show at both the Boston Terrier Club of New York (where he took Reserve Winners) in February 1981 and Best

Am. and Can. Ch. Dan Jee's I'm Suzi Too with the bone that was presented to her when she went Best of Breed at the Boston Terrier Club of Maryland Specialty Show. Owned by the Rosens, Park Ridge, New Jersey.

Puppy in Show at the Boston Terrier Club of Maryland two months later.

Champion Jeffords Scotland Yard Beau was co-bred by the Rosens and Kay Jeffords, being by Champion Jeffords Minute Man ex Champion Jeffords Scotland Yard Lady and born in January 1981, the only puppy in the litter. Quality made up for quantity, however, as the youngster completed championship at just two days over seven months' age, from the puppy class, at Westchester Kennel Club in September 1981, going on to beat the special for Best of Breed. Honore Rosen comments, "I was told by the Parent Club that he was the youngest Boston (male) to ever finish his championship in the history of the breed." Beau has been specialed seven times. During these appearances he has made a Group 2nd win at Holyoke in 1983, and gone Best of Breed at the Boston Terrier Club of Connecticut supported entry at St. Hubert's Kennel Club in July 1985.

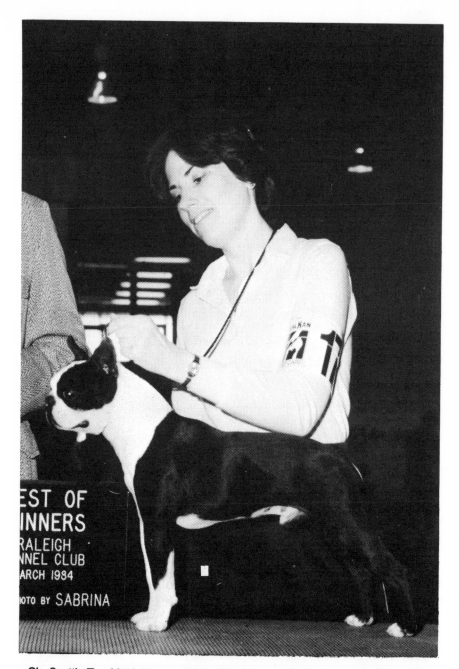

Ch. Scott's Too Much Nonsense, by Ch. Royale Command's Ebony Prince ex Ch. Scott's Stuff N Nonsense, was bred by Barbara Scott and belongs to Susan Watts. Here taking Best of Winners at Raleigh K.C. in March 1984.

SCOTT'S BOSTONS

Barbara Scott at Lillington, North Carolina, is the owner of Scott's Boston Terriers, with whom she has been creating a very lovely and successful line of show quality dogs.

The foundation bitch here appears to be Champion Clasen's Joy, by Champion Toby Junior II ex Clasen's Fantastic Lady. This quality bitch finished in good order, then was bred to Champion El Hi N Star Q's Colonel Botono, a noted Best in Show winner, to produce, among other champions, the well-known Champion Scott's Stuff N Nonsense.

"Pepper," as Stuff N Nonsense is called informally, is the dam of Champion Scott's Just Nonsense, Champion Scott's Too Much Nonsense, Champion Scott's Rhyme N Nonsense, and Champion Scott's Must Be Magic.

The latter Boston, Must Be Magic, is an Australian Non-Sporting Group winner, and the second Boston to be exported to Australia from the United States. In addition she is the dam of a Best in Show puppy in Australia.

Stuff N Nonsense has had impact as a winner as well as a producer with, among other honors, a Non-Sporting Group First from the Bred-by Exhibitor Class under Jane Kay and Best of Breed at the Birmingham Boston Terrier Club Specialty in 1981. She also has more than 30 Best of Breed awards to her credit with approximately 13 Group placements.

SHOWBIZ

Showbiz Boston Terriers, owned by Art and Lil Huddleston, Northridge, California, started in 1958 when this couple purchased the first of their Bostons, who became Champion Gentleman Jim Regardless II. Their first two of the breed, Jim and his daughter Diamond Lil Regardless, carried the strain identification of the Regards and Regardless bloodlines. In 1963, the Huddlestons were the first to use the Showbiz prefix on Champion Showbiz Mr. Chips Regardless, and they have continued to include the "Regardless" whenever possible. The Showbiz prefix was selected as a result of listening to the Walter Winchell broadcasts which he signed off with, "Well, folks, that's Showbiz."

These two Bostons opened a new way of life for the Huddlestons, which included many new friendships and a most engrossing

An outstanding Boston Terrier Puppy, future Ch. Showbiz Rick O'Shay Romance winning at a sanctioned match at exactly six months old. Owner-handled by Art Huddleston for himself and co-owner Lil Huddleston.

Ch. Showbiz Mr. Chips Regardless, famous "star" owned by Arthur and Lillian Huddleston.

and fascinating hobby. As his interest in the breed grew, Art Huddleston began an intensive study into the history of this wonderful breed, leading to his now owning the world's largest collection of Boston Terrier memorabilia, most of its given to them by long-time breeders who no longer had use for it. This prompted Art Huddleston to write, with the result that he has contributed a column to one of the Boston Terrier breed publications, the *Boston Bulletin,* for more than 23 years; and he has written the *Gazette/ Pure-Bred Dogs* breed column bi-monthly since 1976.

Gentleman Jim was the sire of seven champions when he died of nephritis at the young age of seven years. His son, Champion Mr. Chips Regardless, sire of four champions, had, as had Jim, several Bests of Breed and Group placements. Chip's son, Champion Showbiz Rick O Shay Romance, was the sire of ten champions, the last sired, with special permission from the American Kennel Club (required when a stud dog reaches 12 years of age), at age 13 years. Through Rick O Shay Romance, who had many Bests of Breed and Group placements to his credit, the Showbiz line is still producing champions in many of the United States, in Canada, and in England.

The Huddlestons have now retired as breeders but they still own (or are owned by) six Bostons.

Best in Specialty Show at the 1985 Boston Terrier Club of America National. Ch. Staley's El-Bo's Showman, bred and owned by Michael and Beverly Staley.

STALEY

Staley Boston Terriers are owned by Michael and Beverly Staley of Edgewood, Kentucky, who are making quite a name for themselves as outstanding breeders in the Boston Terrier world.

Breeding their lovely bitch, Champion Zodiac's War Witch (by Champion Circus' Candy Man ex Stormy of Bar None) to the widely admired and justly noted Champion El-Bo's Rudy Is A Dandy (Champion Bejays Jim Dandys Happy Guy-Champion El-Bo's Liberty Belle), the Staleys really hit it big with the litter she produced, as three of the puppies grew up to become Champion Staley's El-Bo's Showman, Champion Staley's Trudy Is A Dandy; and Champion El-Bo's Amy Ru, the latter now owned by Eleanor Candland in California.

Both Showman, known to his friends as J.R., and Trudy have remained with their breeders. Showman, as of November 1985, was the No. 1 Boston Terrier in the United States, both Canine Chronicle and Routledge systems; has won the National Specialty in 1985; and is a multiple Best in Show (all breeds) winner. As a sire he is doing equally well, with six puppies who have already become champions, two of them Group winners. Trudy completed title on the same weekend as J.R., and will certainly be a tremendous asset to the Staleys as both a show bitch and a producer. Her dam, War Witch, now has five champions to her credit.

STARTIME

Startime Boston Terriers are owned by Yvette C. Gulledge at Ft. Myers, Florida, who started out with one eight-week-old male puppy. He became Champion Williams Daddies Bigboy Beau, who finished title with natural (uncropped) ears at age nine months with four majors. Then she acquired two bitches, one of which finished with Beau, Champion Williams Velvet Starbaby, a champion at ten months with three majors; the other the litter sister to Beau's dam, Gleeson's Miz Petunia. This older bitch also gained some championship points. These three Bostons comprised the foundation stock for Startime Kennels.

Starbaby was bred to Beau, resulting in one male pup who became Champion Williams Command Stormboy. Starbaby was completely linebred into Beau's background, and the results of this breeding were very satisfactory. Miz Petunia (Tammy) was then bred to Beau, his dam's litter sister, producing a dog, Champion Williams Velvet Blueboy (finished with four majors), and a small bitch puppy, Williams Velvet Bonnie, who earned ten points.

Next Starbaby was bred to Blueboy, bringing forth a litter which contained four puppies, all of whom gained title: Champion Williams The Boston Blackie (title completed at age one year); Champion Williams Startime Bambi (finished at age seven months); Champion Williams Startime Bluebelle (gained title at 11 months); and Champion Williams Startime Starbrite, the most recent to have finished.

At that time a straight genetically bred line of three stud champions was maintained.

Startime Bostons are now into fourth and fifth generations from Blackie and his get being bred, shown and finished. Owner Yvette Gulledge is now in the process of backbreeding to grandsires and great-grandsires and dams. She comments, "I have had very few anomalies (two splashed and one white hemisphere in markings), one domed head, and one butterfly nose."

Champion Williams Daddies Bigboy Beau, best Veteran at the Miami Specialty with many wins to his credit, is now retired and the many bitches who are sent to him are having consistently good

Ch. Stormcrest Mr. Carry On, by Ch. ML's Call Me Mister ex Ch. Stormcrest Carrie Carry On, completed championship as a puppy with all major wins, finishing by taking Best of Winners at the Tri Angle Specialty. Owned by Stormcrest Bostons, D.M. Sotack.

Ch. Williams Startime Bambi, by Ch. Williams Velvet Blueboy ex Ch. Williams Velvet Starbaby, is a multiple Best of Breed and Group-placing homebred. Handled by Yvette Williams Gulledge.

show get. Beau is a 14 ½″ perfectly marked and very dominant dog.

Champion Williams Velvet Blue and Champion Williams Command Stormboy are also dominant sires, putting out small, sturdy, exceptionally well-gaited puppies.

Champion Williams The Boston Blackie is now being used extensively and is siring show quality pups. Both fourth and fifth generation youngsters are now being readied for the circuits.

STORMCREST

Stormcrest Boston Terriers are owned by D.M. Sotack, and are situated at Weatherly, Pennsylvania.

The owner of this kennel has been active in the Boston Terrier world for about 28 years (since the late 1960's) and has built an impressive record as a breeder. In 1985 alone, five championships have been completed for "Stormcrest," including three puppies winning at Specialty Shows.

Champion Stormcrest Mr. Carry On is one of the 1985 group to finish. Homebred and owned by M.L. Zimmerman, he is by Champion M L's Call Me Mister ex Champion Stormcrest Carrie Carry On.

SUNWOODS

Sunwoods Boston Terriers have become synonymous with top quality Boston Terriers, thanks to the interest and efforts of Jill Ritchey and her husband, Dr. Robert Ritchey, DVM, of Canal Fulton, Ohio.

Although Sunwood was originally established in 1942 by Jill's parents, Mr. and Mrs. John Harig, breeding Boxers was the activity there in those days, and Jill showed and helped to raise many a fine dog in that breed. Following her marriage to Bob, they decided that they wanted to work with a smaller breed, and in 1978 Bob presented Jill with Alexandra's Star Reward.

"Luke," as he is lovingly called, finished his American championship while still a puppy. While awaiting confirmation of this fact from A.K.C., Luke discovered and moved on to the bed, promptly reaching the decision that show life was not his bag, but that home living and girl friends were the real thing.

After the purchase of Luke, the Ritcheys visited Andy Turner and the famed Tops Again Boston kennels, from where they purchased two excellent bitches with which to establish their breeding program. Both gained their championships, then went on to prove their value from the whelping box. At this same time, Jill became friends with Tom Enwright, owner of the Good Time Bostons, from whom she purchased the handsome Champion Good Times Leroy T. Brown. Leroy led the kennel until such time as Luke reached the age to take over his share of the stud work. Thus the foundation of Sunwoods Bostons was laid on the lines of Good Times and Tops Again, a combination with which Jill has produced 27 homebred champions in seven short years.

The famed Champion Milady Deacon of Boston was sold by Mr. Enwright, but the new owners did not like her. Upon getting her back, he offered her to Jill as a "possible brood bitch." The rest is history, as from the moment she arrived, Jill and her handler Jerry Rigden realized that there was a special quality Lady possessed, and at her very first show she proved them to be correct. Lady romped through her championship, and in record time

Ch. Sunwoods Reflection, by Ch. Alexander's Star Reward ex Sunwoods Cupie Doll, was bred by Jill Ritchey and is owned by Dr. and Mrs. Robert Ritchey. Winning points towards title, handled by Elaine Rigden under noted Canadian all-breed judge Mrs. Doris Wilson.

had become No. 1 Boston Terrier Bitch in the country. She was shown consistently against all competition, defeating the tops in both sexes in the country at one time or another. Her many, many Group and Best in Show awards were gained over numerous great and outstanding dogs being campaigned in other breeds at this same time.

Sunwoods has produced a series of champions consisting of Ch. Sunwoods Charlie Son, Ch. Sunwoods Merry Munchin, Ch. Sunwoods Reflection, Ch. Sunwoods California Boy, Ch. Sunwoods Show Boat, Ch. Sunwoods Most Rewarding, Ch. Sunwoods Rewarding Star, Ch. Sunwoods Whimsical Winston, Ch. Sunwoods Lookin Good, Ch. Sunwoods Show N'Tell, Ch. Sunwoods Star Attraction, Ch. Sunwoods Lil Darlin, Ch. Sunwoods Bit O'Brandy, Ch. Sunwoods Stormy Ann, Ch. Sunwoods Classic Design, Ch. Sunwoods Oreo Cookie, Ch. Sunwoods Chief of Staff, Ch. Sunwoods Sweet Tradition, Ch. Jill Woody, Ch. Bob Bull

Left: Ch. Talone's Pilot Lite of Torchy. *Right:* Talone's Play Bunny. *Bottom:* Ch. Talone's Paper Doll, get of the above, John and Nancy Talone, breeders-owners.

Ch. Talone's Tried-N-True, by Ch. Byron's TNT ex Ch. Talone's Topper-N-Tina, finishing title with a three-point major, Winners Dog and Best of Winners at Greater Daytona D.F.A. in 1979. Owner-handled by Nancy Talone for herself and John Talone.

Woody, Ch. Bluette Cool Hand Luke, Ch. Mindy Mite of Little Acres, Ch. Blazermins Nicole of Sunwoods, and Ch. Lynndales Mr. T.

Luke continues a top producer and is second only to the now deceased great Champion Zodiac's Special Beau. His progeny and others carrying the Sunwoods prefix are now the foundation of new kennels from Maine to California, and in 1985 Jill Ritchey was named Breeder of the Year by the Boston Terrier Club of America, a very big honor for so young a kennel, and at the same time extremely well deserved. However, Jill's greatest pride and pleasure is the fact that Sunwoods, along with continuing to breed and show Bostons themselves, has sold top quality Bostons to new breeders and exhibitors. Thus on any given weekend, a Sunwoods Boston may well be in the purple in several different shows across the United States and in Canada which is really exciting for this truly dedicated breeder!

TALONE'S

Talone's Boston Terriers are the result of John and Nancy Talone, of Knoxville, Tennessee, having in 1969 purchased two members of the breed: Talone's Special Pug and Talone's Play Bunny. They in due course were bred for the first time, producing in that litter a bitch called Talone's Tippy Toes, who herself, when bred to Hilton's Little Sparky Boy (Showman bloodlines) became the dam of Champion Talone's Anniversary Girl — the second champion to be finished by the Talones and the first homebred. Actually both Girl and the lovely Champion Talone's Topper-N-Tina were campaigned during the same period, both finishing with Topper-N-Tina, bred by Lucille Sheets, slightly ahead of the homebred Girl.

Topper-N-Tina, by Champion Thomas Main Topper ex Tina Marie X, combines TNT, B.B. and Good News lines. A consistent multiple breed and Group winner, she is also the dam of two champions, the result of a breeding back to her grandsire, Champion Byron's TNT. These are Champion Talone's Tried and True and Champion Talone's Tisket-N-Tasket, both multiple breed and Specialty winners; Tried-N-True is the sire of champions.

Champion Talone's Pilot Lite of Torchy, by Champion Torchy's Good News of Sunglo (Sunglo, Regardless bloodlines) ex Cheer-

On Mi-Lady (B.B. and Command bloodlines), bred by Lucille Sheets, was the Talones' first male champion to finish. A multiple breed winner, he also sired four champions.

The original Iowana bitch bred to Pilot, Champion Talone's Paper Doll, was the dam of champions and a multiple breed winner.

Another cross between TNT and Sunglo bloodlines led to Champion Talone's Ruff-N-Tuff, a multiple breed winner and the sire of the exciting Champion Talone's Sugar-N-Spice whom they consider to be the best of their current champions.

Sugar-N-Spice, the product of TNT and Sunglo breeding, was crossed with the original bloodlines of Iowana by breeding a granddaughter of the two original Talone Bostons. This was the breeding which produced Sugar-N-Spice, her parents being Ruff-N-Tuff and Talone's Bittersweet Memory. Sugar, with many breed and Group successes, really pleased her breeder-owners when she took Best of Opposite Sex at the Cincinnati Specialty in 1984, the event at that date holding the record entry for Boston Specialties.

The younger generation at Talone's consists of Talone's Put-N-On the Ritz, Talone's Ruff-N-Ready II and Talone's Rise-N-Shine, who are by Ruff-N-Tuff ex Talone's Special Beau Brandy.

TRU-MARK

Tru-Mark Boston Terriers are owned by Mrs. Dorothy Truman at Rockbridge Baths, Virginia. This kennel is based upon the Clasen bloodlines, and is dedicated to both obedience and conformation Bostons.

Foundation bitch here is Champion Clasen's Cherub, C.D., a daughter of Champion Toby Junior II ex Clasen's Cindy Lou (daughter of Champion Clasen's Honey Moon Junior). After completing her championship in good order, she was bred, in due time becoming the dam of several champions, as all of her puppies who were shown completed their titles.

For herself, Mrs. Truman kept Champion R.T.'s Cricket of Tru-Mark, C.D. whom she took through to both titles. It is a source of pride to all concerned that a littermate to Cricket, Champion Buster of Tru-Mark owned by Robert Marvel, Lancaster, Pennsylvania, completed his bench show title at the American Kennel Club Centennial Dog Show during November of 1984.

Ch. What's Up Tiger Lily, by Am. and Can. Ch. Kimkev's Sundance Kid, ex Apollo's Flashing Fancy, was bred by Judy Griffith who is co-owner with Maxine Uzoff.

MAXINE UZOFF

Maxine Uzoff of Houston, Texas, is one of the newer breeders who has become thoroughly "sold" on Boston Terriers and hopes to breed many good ones in the future.

Maxine started in the mid-1970's when she purchased her first one as a pet. A few years after that a second one joined her family. The latter was definitely breeding quality, and perhaps it was fate that brought her into heat right at the time of the Houston Astro Dog Show cluster! For there Marilyn saw what seemed to her the ideal dog to whom her bitch should be bred. He was named Kimkev's Sundance Kid, and at that time he had just started out and was quite immature, being only just one year of age. His handler, Judy Webb, agreed with Maxine Uzoff that the two should be bred, and through her patience and effort in bringing it about, a gorgeous little daughter was eventually born.

She is Champion What's Up Tiger Lily, and she is a real credit to her now-famous sire who went on to become an American and Canadian Champion and a Top Ten Boston in 1982 and 1983.

Maxine Uzoff is very happy to have such a lovely bitch as Tiger Lily to start her off in the Boston Terrier world. She also is appreciative of the friends she has made in the Boston fancy and their helpfulness.

Ch. Scotts Too Much Nonsense, owned by Susan Watts, pictured on the way to the title in February 1985.

WATTSES

Wattses Quality Bostons at Lexington, North Carolina, are owned by a new fancier of the breed, Susan Watts, whose parents had been owners of quality pet Bostons throughout her youth. By the time she had decided to raise them, she could not afford to purchase what she considered to be truly top quality, so she had to start at the beginning to breed up from what she could buy, using the handsome champions belonging to Clara Phillips who encouraged her by permitting Susan to use them on her bitches.

Susan was familiar with and liked the Clasen line, so she tried to stay within it, and still does. She linebred Champion Danjee's Dapper Dan progeny and as close relatives of his as she could find. Champion Scott's Stuff N' Nonsense is of Clasen breeding very similar to Dapper Dan, as she found by a study of their pedigrees. She had a son by Champion Royal Command Ebony Prince of the strong foundation Command line. Susan bought this fine male from his breeder, Barbara Scott, and had him shown by Johnny and Patricia Johnson. Now he has completed his title, becoming Champion Scott's Too Much Nonsense.

Susan's hopes now are centered around a lovely puppy by this dog from Wattses Blue Moon Treasure, who will soon start out for her championship. She will be known as Wattses Sunny Perfection, and the eventual plan is to breed her to a fine stud from the Clasen line when the time comes.

YOKI-EN

Yoki-En Boston Terriers are owned by Mary and Alice Ochiai at Glendale, California.

These ladies are the owners of a very special brood bitch whom they call "Debbie," who is officially Standup-N-Cheer, the dam

Ch. Sir Whiff-N-Poof taking Best of Breed at Sir Francis Drake K.C., April 1984. Bred and owned by Mary and Alice Ochiai and handled by Michael Dougherty. Born in 1982, this is a son of Ch. El-Bo's Rudy ex Standup-N-Cheer, also bred and owned by Mary and Alice Ochiai.

93

of four lovely champions in two litters (one of them a Canadian champion), and who had recently been bred to Champion Rudy Is A Dandy.

As a show bitch, in between litters, "Debbie," as a puppy, won the Pasadena Boston Terrier Club Sweepstakes, and she has championship points along with being about to embark on a career in obedience. She is the dam of Champion Sir Whiff-N-Poof, Champion Little Miss Goodie, Champion Yoki-En's Miss Night-N-Gale, and Champion El-Bo's Puttin' on the Ritz, all sired by Dandy.

Champion Sir Whiff-N-Poof was exclusively owner-handled to his championship by his breeder, who is now also campaigning him as a special, although he is sometimes handled in the latter competition by Alvin N. Lee, Jr. His show record stands at 25 times Best of Breed, three Group placements, three Specialty wins including two successively at Golden Gate Boston Terrier Club, and various others. He is also making his presence felt as a sire, with some future champion type puppies at present getting ready to go.

Champion Little Miss Goodie recently had her first litter, sired by Champion Staley's El-Bo's Showman, and is now returning successfully to the ring following these maternal duties. She made her title with ease, and has some prestigious Best of Opposite Sex awards to her credit at this time.

Champion Yoki-En's Miss Night-N-Gale became a champion at only nine months of age, handled by Alvin Lee, Jr. She now has several Best of Breed awards and some Bests of Opposite Sex. She is the first of the Ochiai-owned Bostons to carry their new Yo-ki-En kennel prefix, to which she is definitely a credit. Her litter brother, Champion El-Bo's Puttin' on the Ritz, has already gained championship status in both the United States and Canada.

ZODIAC

Zodiac Boston Terriers, at Des Moines, Iowa, belong to Juanita B. Camp, and dogs from here are among the most famous and admired of this breed.

The kennel started with Vogel's Velvet Cover Girl, a nine pound female by Champion Victor of Bar None, who was then bred to Champion Unique's Royalty Kid. This breeding produced Cham-

Ch. Zodiac's Special Warrior is by Ch. Zodiac's Special Beau ex Ch. Zodiac's War Witch. Photo courtesy of breeder, Juanita Camp. Zodiac Boston Terriers.

pion Unique's Star of Zodiac, who, bred back to Champion U-nique's Special Beau, became the dam of Champion Zodiac's Special Beau.

Another female at this then new kennel was Stormy of Bar None, whom Juanita bred to Champion Circus's Candy Man. From this came Champion Zodiac's War Witch, who in her turn, bred back to Champion Zodiac's Special Beau, produced Champion Zodiac's Special Warrior. Later War Witch was sold to the Staleys, who bred her to Champion El-Bo's Rudy Is A Dandy, thus producing Champion Staley's El-Bo's Showman.

Juanita Camp comments that she is proud to have had the good sense to realize that Bob Breum could do more than she would have been able to by way of making Champion Zodiac's Special Beau a famous dog. She adds that to her, it is always a complete mystery why people will raise a really spectacular dog with great potential, which they know they will be unable to campaign as they should, and refuse to part with it to someone who could do so. Many such people lack the showring talent to make the most of a dog and present him to best advantage, yet adamantly refuse to part with that dog for any amount of money because he *is* so

Ch. Zodiac's Star of Unique, littermate to Ch. Unique's Star of Zodiac (Special Beau's dam), taking Winners Bitch at the Minnesota Boston Terrier Club in 1978. Mary Harris handling for owner Juanita Camp.

good. How much wiser it is, under those circumstances, to let such a dog go where he will be in a position to achieve the recognition his quality deserves. That way the breeder profits by general acknowledgement of the dog's superior attributes and the breed profits by another outstanding representative in the show ring.

We salute Juanita Camp as an outstanding breeder and as a lady of practical common sense.

← Overleaf:

Ch. Alexander's Star Reward, by Ch. Star Ho's Prince Valiant ex Alexander Di Lie Dot-T. Owned by Dr. and Mrs. Robert Ritchey. Bred by Linda Alexander.

1. Ch. Alexander's Magic Wanda, by Ch. Alexander's Rose Royce ex Alexander's Country Gal, pictured winning Best of Breed under Jane Kay on the way to winning Group 1st from the Puppy Class. A most elegant and eye-appealing Boston owned by the Alexanders, Waynesboro, Georgia.

2. Ch. Bo-K's Hey Look Me Over, by Ch. Bo-K's Nu Masterpiece of Model ex Ch. Bo-K's Special Model of Balboa is the dam of two champions. Bred and owned by Bob and Karen Milham, Bo-K Bostons, Phoenix, Arizona.

3. Ch. Alexander's Sweet Treat, by Ch. Alexander's Rose Royce ex Alexander's Polka Dot, a beautiful red brindle bitch with a great love of dog shows. One of the many outstanding Boston Terriers owned by Jim and Linda Alexander, Waynesboro Georgia.

4. Best Brace in Show, San Diego K.C., Ch. Bonnie's Rock-N-Roar and Ch. Bonnie's Sugar-N-Spice, by Ch. Byron's T-N-T ex Bonnie's Sweetheart O'Showbiz, C.D.X. Bred and owned by Rita Otteson and Mae Wiger, Anaheim, California.

5. Ch. Bo-K's Nu Masterpiece of Model, by Mex. and Am. Ch. Balboa Handsome Model ex Ch. Sage 'n Sand Nu Toi Tu. The sire of nine champions, this handsome dog was bred, owned, and handled by Bob and Karen Milham, Phoenix, Arizona.

6. Ch. Alexander's Dear Abby, a daughter of Ch. Alexander's Rose Royce ex Alexander's Double Dot-T. In 1983 she was Winners Bitch and Best of Opposite Sex at the Birmingham Specialty. She is the dam of Ch. Alexander's Dear John, who was sired by Ch. Zodiac Special Beau. Linda and Jim Alexander, Alexander Bostons, Waynesboro, Georgia.

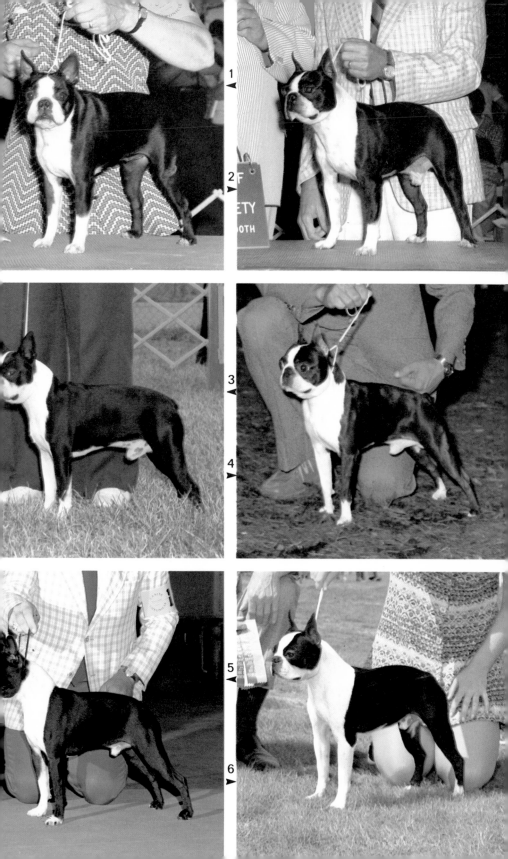

← Overleaf:

1. Ch. Chahary Besame Mucho Ballade, breeder-owned and handled by Ira Smoluchowski, Chahary Kennels, Rockford, Illinois. By Ch. Sabe's Circus Punchinello ex Ch. Chahary Une Baiser Moi Kismet.

2. Ch. Blazer of Top's Agaan going Best of Breed, owner-handled by Jim Cronen, Louisville, Kentucky. Sired by Ch. Hi-Ark's Rocky O'Neil ex Madam Sheilas Butterfly.

3. Am., Can., Bda., and Venez. Ch. Chahary Crown Prince, by Ch. Unique's Royalty Kid ex Ch. Chahary Beau-K Lalka Karima. Bred by Ira Smoluchowski, Chahary Kennels, Rockford, Illinois; owned by Ed Luther. Pictured winning Group 2nd at La Porte K.C. in 1979.

4. Ch. Byron's Show-N-Tell, by Bonnie's Lord Byron ex Cheri's Precious Bunnie, owned by Doris and Byron Munson, North Hollywood, California.

5. Am. and Can. Ch. Chahary Orante Ri Owen winning Best of Breed at Kenosha in September 1983. Owned by Mary McMahon, bred by Ira Smoluchowski. This is a son of Mike Mar's Oxford Square from Ch. Chahary Cristenelli.

6. Ch. Byron's Bib-N-Tucker going on to Best of Breed from the classes at Santa Ana. One of the outstanding Bostons from this famous kennel of the Byrons. Handled by Melody Stoltz.

1. Ch. Clasen's Toby's Profile, son of Ch. Toby Junior II ex Shani Wynter Brooke, finished in July 1976 at Wallkill K.C. Owned by Mrs. Harry N. Clasen, Mechanicville, New York.

2. Cia's Brandy's Best Beau at age eight months, winning Best of Breed at Suffolk County in 1985. Mrs. Anita G. Ciannilli, owner, Syracuse, New York.

3. Future Ch. Country Kin Tony Award at eight months old making his show debut owner-handled by Warren Uberroth, Staten Island, New York, by taking Winners Dog at the Boston Terrier Club of Connecticut Specialty, September 1984. An outstanding young dog who should contribute much to his breed.

4. Ch. El-Bo's Amy Ru, homebred daughter of Ch. El-Bo's Rudy Is A Dandy, carrying on in the winning family tradition. Eleanor and Bob Candland, El-Bo Bostons, Lake Elsinore, California.

5. Ch. El-Bo's Amy Ru, a daughter of Ch. El-Bo's Rudy Is A Dandy, another lovely homebred owned by Eleanor and Bob Candland, Lake Elsinore, California.

6. Ch. El-Bo's Rudy Is A Dandy winning one of his close to 90 Group Firsts. Breeder-owner-handled, as always, by Bob Candland, Lake Elsinore, California.

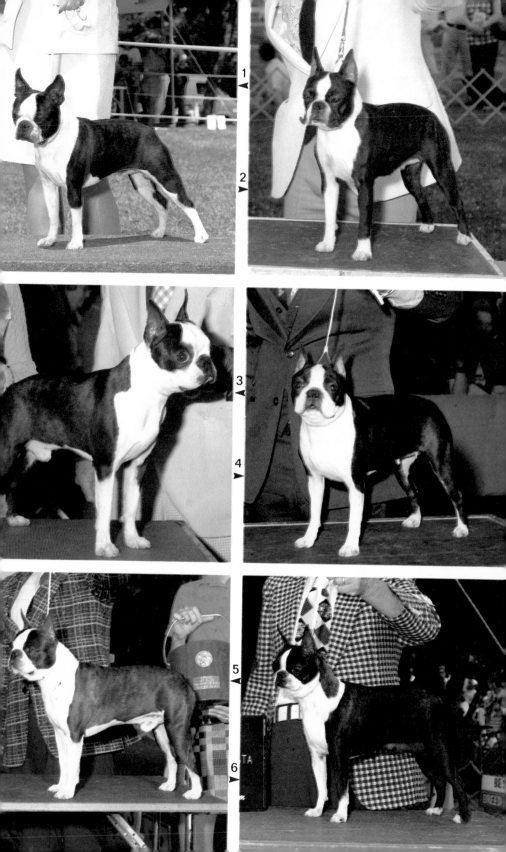

← Overleaf:

1. Ch. Fraser's Merry Minstrelman, by Ch. McGee's Jason of Sacto ex Fraser's Elegant Tuf Teena, winning Best of Breed, Rogue Valley K.C. 1985. Bred, owned, and handled by Lois Fraser, Sacramento, California.

2. Ch. Jeffords Constance as a mature bitch making one of her many prestigious wins—Best Non-Sporting Dog. Constance handled by Michael Wolf for himself and Mrs. Walter Jeffords.

3. Ch. Good Time Jody T. Brown, son of Ch. Good Time Charlie T. Brown ex Ch. B-B's Toya's Tanya, is the sire of three champions, including the fabulous Ch. Milady Beacon of Boston who is owned by Mrs. Jill Ritchey. Jody T. Brown is one of the Good Time Bostons, Thomas L. Enwright, Winter Haven, Florida.

4. The famous Best in Show bitch, Ch. Jefford's Abigail, winning the breed at Westminster in 1978 for Mrs. Walter M. Jeffords and Michael Wolf who handled. A famed all-breed Best in Show, multi-Group and Specialty Show winner.

5. Ch. Good Time Charlie T. Brown winning one of his numerous Non-Sporting Group awards, owner-handled by Thomas L. Enwright, Winter Haven, Florida.

6. Ch. Good Times Tanya's Toy, sired by Am. and Can. Ch. Chahary Adonis Jovan out of Ch. B-B's Toya's Tanya. This lovely bitch winning points at Jupiter-Requesta in April 1981, is a homebred and handled by Thomas L. Enwright, Winter Haven, Florida.

1. Ch. Zodiac's Star of Victory, by Ch. Unique's Judge's Choice ex Ch. Unique's Star of Zodiac, bred by Juanita Camp and owned by Leonard L. Myers, Denver, Colorado.

2. The famed Ch. Jefford's Abigail, then co-owned by Mrs. Walter M. Jeffords and Michael Wolf adding still another to her long list of Group victories at Back Mountain K.C. in 1976. One of the immortals of this breed, Abigail blazed a trail of glory through the important Eastern Dog Shows.

3. Ch. Maestro's Special Tootsie, by Ch. Zodiac's Special Beau ex Maestro's Sonata By Reporter, while still competing in the classes. Owned by Julius (Jay) Martell, Maestro Bostons, Topeka, Kansas.

4. Ch. Iowana's Miracle Kid, by Ch. Command's Miracle ex Iowana's Desert Dawn, owned by Leonard L. Myers, Denver, Colorado. Bred by Florence M. Dancer.

5. Ch. Iowana's Fancy Danette, by Ch. Sage'n'Sand Have Tux Will Travel ex Iowana's Desert Dawn, was bred by Florence M. Dancer. Owner, Leonard L. Myers, Kingway Bostons, Denver, Colorado.

6. Regal Legacy Brenda La Star, owned by Wade S. Burns and Jon Woodring, Lanbur Kennels, Advance, North Carolina, has 14 points including three majors. One of these wins is pictured here at Kennesaw K.C. May 1985.

← **Overleaf:**

1. Unique Pleasure Riva, by Ch. Staley's El-Bo's Showman ex Am. and Can. Ch. Unique Pleasure Lacy, pictured at her first match show when exactly three months old. She will be well into her show career and has already an all-breed Best Puppy in Match to her credit. Owners, Ed and Cindy Galor, Lisle, Illinois.

2. Ch. Albelarm Special Too, owned by Mrs. Alan Robson, Albelarm Kennels and Michael Wolf, Mike Mar Kennels. Another outstanding winner for the breed. Winning a Group First here in 1985 Southern Maryland K.C.

3. Another famous Boston Terrier co-owned and handled by Michael Wolf, this is Ch. Albelarm Rather Special who here is winning Best of Breed at Westminster in 1983. This son of Ch. Zodiac's Special Beau ex Ch. Maestro's Animato By Reporter, was bred by Julius Martell and is owned by Mr. Wolf with Mrs. Alan Robson. Mr. Wolf's Mike Mar Bostons are at Oxford, Pennsylvania.

4. Ch. Albelarm Rather Special, owned by Mrs. Alan Robson and Michael Wolf, is a consistent winner in hottest Eastern Non-Sporting Group competition. Pictured in 1982 winning Best of Breed at Carroll County.

5. Ch. Maestro's Sophie's Choice, born April 1983, owned by Mary Alice Niebauer and shown to the title by Joseph Niebauer. Now, under Jerry Rigden's handling, she has become a multiple Group winner with nine such victories to her credit by November 1985. Bred by Jay Martell of Topeka, Kansas, she is a daughter of Ch. Zodiac's Special Beau ex Maestro's Sonata. Here winning the Group at Western Pennsylvania in 1985. The Niebauers are from Cassopolis, Michigan.

6. The noted Group-winning Ch. Maestro's Kool Kid Miff here is taking Best Non-Sporting Dog at Maryland Kennel Club in 1984. This dog was one of the Top Ten Bostons in the United States according to *Canine Chronicle,* October 30, 1985. Owned at the time by Willie Mae and Julius "Jay" Martell, Topeka, Kansas.

1. Ch. Country Kin's Carmelina winning the Non-Sporting Group at Riverhead Kennel Club in 1981. Handled by co-owner, Mrs. Honore Rosen, Scotland Yard Bostons, Park Ridge, New Jersey.

2. Regal Legacy Stars N Stripes, by Am. and Can. Ch. Simon's Hihope Mr. Hobo ex Ch. Regal Legacy No Finah Dinah, starting her career with Best of Winners at James River K.C. in 1985. Handled by co-owner Jose F. Negron for himself and Anthony A. Antolics, Regal Legacy Bostons, Annandale, Virginia.

3. Ch. Schubo's Inspirin' Candidate, by Ch. Candidate's Roving Reporter ex Royale Show Man's Mona Lisa was bred by Pearl Ruble and was one of the foundation Bostons at Schubo Kennels, Wes and Karen Schultz, Amarillo, Texas.

4. Ch. Regal Legacy Cisco The Kid, by Am. and Can. Ch. Simms Hihope Mr. Hobo ex Regal Legacy Lady Vanessa, was bred by Anthony A. Antolics and Jose F. Negron, Annandale, Virginia. Mr. Negron handled this Boston to a Best of Breed win at Virginia Kennel Club in 1984.

5. Ch. Jeffords Scotland Yard Beau, by Ch. Jeffords Minute Man ex Ch. Jeffords Scotland Yard Lady, was bred by Marc and Honore Rosen, owners, Park Ridge, New Jersey, and by Mrs. Kay Jeffords. Pictured placing Group 2nd at Holyoke K.C. 1983. Owner-handled by Honore Rosen.

6. Ch. Country Kin Scotland Yard Ace, by Ch. B.B.'s Dudes Little Hobo ex Country Kin Auntie Mame, winning Best Puppy in Show at the Boston Terrier Club of Maryland on April 11, 1981. Owner-handled by Honore Rosen, Scotland Yard Boston Terriers, Park Ridge, New Jersey.

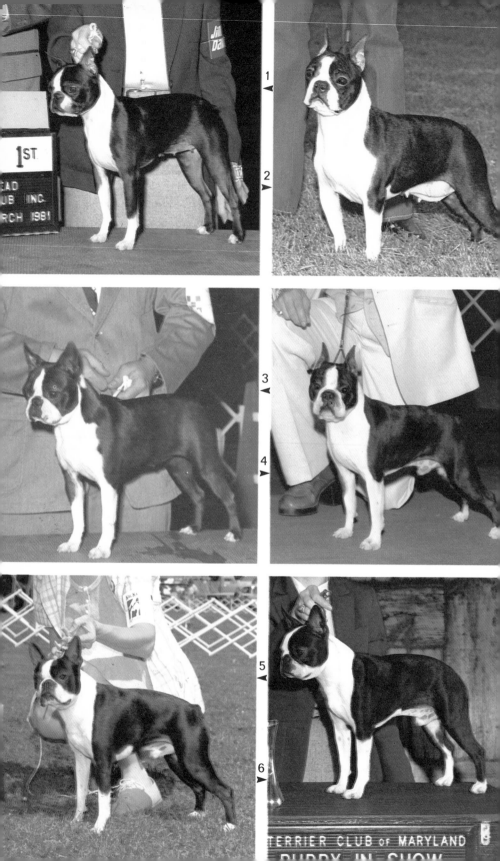

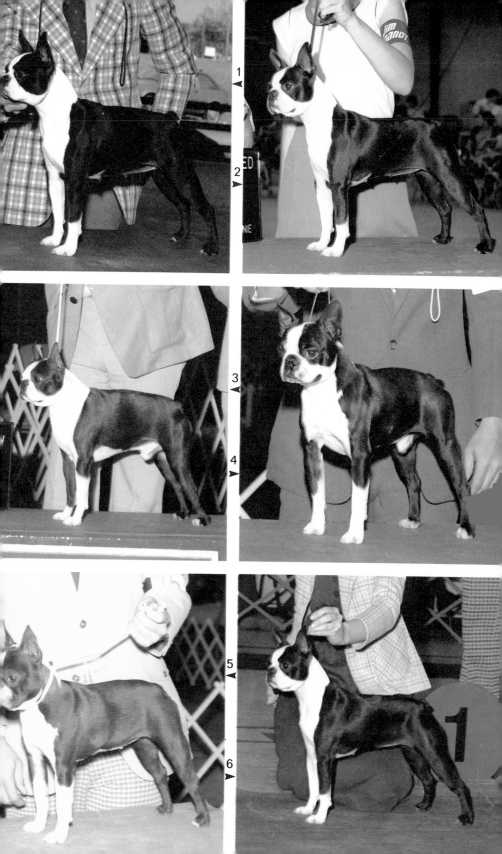

← **Overleaf:**

1. Ch. Scott's Stuff N Nonsense, owned by Barbara Scott, Lillington, North Carolina—a Group and Specialty winning bitch by Best in Show Ch. El Hi N Star Q's Colonel Botono ex Ch. Clasen's Joy, taking a Best of Breed under judge Wilma Hunter in 1981, handled by Jon Woodring. This bitch has more than 50 Bests of Breed and about 25 Group placements.

2. Ch. Scott's Stuff N Nonsense, by Ch. El Hi N Star Q's Colonel Botono ex Ch. Clasen's Joy. "Pepper" here has just won Best of Breed from the classes over specials, the judge on this occasion being Mrs. Parker Grant. Bred and owned by Barbara Scott, Scott's Bostons at Lillington, North Carolina.

3. Another all-breed Best in Show for Ch. Staley's El-Bo's Showman, this time at Nashville, K.C., September 1984. As always, handled by co-breeder/owner (with Beverly Staley) Michael Staley, Edgewood, Kentucky.

4. Ch. Schubo's Streakin' Sky Rocket, by Ch. Schubo's Roamin' Romance ex Ch. Schubo's Inspirin' Candidate, one of the noted homebreds owned by Wes and Karen Schultz, Schubo's Boston Terriers, Amarillo, Texas.

5. Ch. Schubo's Flashin' Gold Dust, bred by Ralph Vogel by Ch. Unique's Gay Beau ex Vogel's Showman's Flashette. Finished with three majors in 1976, this was the first of the champions at Schubo's Kennels, Wes and Karen Schultz, Amarillo, Texas.

6. The noted Ch. Scott's Stuff N Nonsense, bred and owned by Barbara Scott of Scott's Boston Terriers, pictured here winning the Non-Sporting Group after coming up from the Bred-by-Exhibitor Class at Durham in 1979 under judge Jane Kay. The dam of champions, including one who is helping to establish correct type in Australia.

1. Ch. Sunwoods Most Rewarding, by Ch. Alexander Star Reward ex Top's Again's Happy Princess. Bred and owned by Dr. and Mrs. Robert Ritchey, Canal Fulton, Ohio.

2. Ch. Talone's Tisket-N-Tasket, by Ch. Byron's TNT ex Ch. Talone's Topper-N-Tina, winning a 5-point major at the Boston Terrier Club of Greater Cincinnati Specialty, May 1980. The judge was Ray Perso, Peter Baynes handled for owners John and Nancy Talone, Knoxville, Tennesse.

3. Ch. Sunwoods Show N'Tell, by Ch. Alexander Star Reward ex Sunwoods Lady Dyanna, at Rubber City K.C. in 1984. Handled by Jerry Rigden for Dr. and Mrs. Robert Ritchey, breeders/owners, Sunwoods Bostons, Canal Fulton, Ohio.

4. Ch. Buttons of Tops Again Ace, by Ch. Tops Again Ace ex Pomeroy Miss Iffie. Bred by Felicia Pomeroy. Owned by Dr. and Mrs. Robert Ritchey, Canal Fulton, Ohio.

5. Ch. Talone's Topper-N-Tina (by Ch. Byron's TNT ex Tina Maria) completing her title at Carolina K.C. in March 1976, taking Winners Bitch and Best of Opposite Sex from the author. Bred by Lucille Sheets, handled by Peter Baynes for owners, John and Nancy Talone, Knoxville, Tennessee.

6. Ch. Staley's Trudy Is A Dandy, littermate to Ch. Staley's El-Bo's Showman, finished title on the same weekend as her brother, at the Louisville Specialty in 1984. Handled by Michael Staley, Edgewood, Kentucky, for himself and Beverly Staley, breeders-owners of these two exciting Bostons.

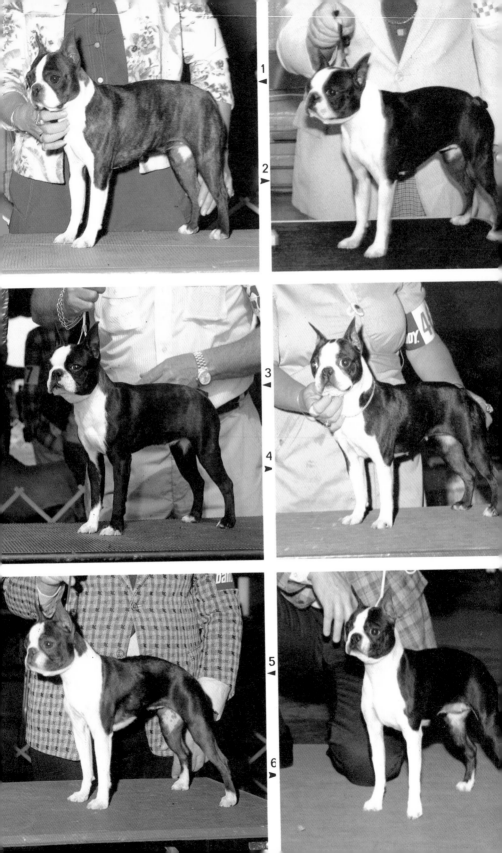

1. Ch. Zodiac's War Witch taking Winners Bitch and Best of Opposite Sex for a 3-point major at the Boston Terrier Club of Topeka 1980. Witch, by Ch. Circus Candy Man ex Stormy of Bar None, was bred and handled by Juanita Camp and is the dam of Ch. Zodiac's Special Warrior and Ch. Staley's El-Bo's Showman.

2. Famous professional handler Judy Webb is among the folks who love and appreciate Boston Terriers. Here she is holding Ch. What's Up Tiger Lily *(left)* and Tiger Lily's sire, Am. and Can. Ch. Kimkev's Sundance Kid *(right)*. Tiger Lily was bred by Judy Griffith who co-owns her with Maxine Uzoff. Sundance Kid was bred by Betty Swick and is owned by Peggy Clark, M.D., Albuquerque, New Mexico. Kid was one of the Top Ten Bostons for 1982 and 1983, handled by Judy Webb. Photo courtesy of Maxine Uzoff.

3. Ch. Zodiac's Star of Victory, by Ch. Unique's Judge's Choice ex Ch. Unique's Star of Zodiac, is a half sister to Ch. Zodiac's Special Beau. Bred by Juanita Camp. Owned by Leonard Myers.

4. Ch. Zodiac's Mandy of Bar None is by Ch. Victor of Bar None ex Stormy of Bar None. Bred, owned, and handled by Juanita Camp, Zodiac Bostons, Des Moines, Iowa.

5. Ch. Little Miss Goodie, daughter of the famous Ch. El-Bo's Rudy Is A Dandy ex Standup-N-Cheer (like Miss Goodie, homebred and owned by Mary and Alice Ochiai, Glendale, California). Pictured taking Best of Opposite Sex handled by owner-breeder at Los Encinos K.C., December 1983.

6. Standup-N-Cheer winning Best in Sweepstakes at the Boston Terrier Sweepstakes, Pasadena Boston Terrier Club Specialty Show, May 1981. A show star, "Debbie" is also being trained for a career in obedience. Owned by Mary K. and Alice S. Ochiai, Glendale, California.

1. Ch. Sunwood's Sweet Reward, by Ch. Alexander Star Reward ex Sun-woods' Cupie Doll, going Best of Opposite Sex at Delaware, Ohio, in April 1984. Owner-handled by Jim Cronen, Louisville, Kentucky.

2. Ch. Good Time Charlie's Angel by Ch. Good Time Charlie T. Brown ex Ch. B.B.'s Toya's Tanya, handled by Elaine Rigden to a Group 2nd under the author. Owned by Dr. and Mrs. Robert Ritchey, Canal Fulton, Ohio. Bred by Thomas L. Enwright.

3. Ch. Bo-K's Limited Edition, by Ch. J.R.'s Chief Petty Officer ex Bo-K's Whim of Elgance, was bred by Bob and Karen Milham and is owned by William and Margaret Preston, Rub'n Buff Bostons, Phoenix, Arizona. Lim-ited Edition was Winners Dog at the 1983 Valley of the Sun Boston Terrier Club, winner of a 5-point major, and finished with a total of four major wins for 19 points.

4. Ch. Byron's Show-N-Tell with owner Doris Munson who has just handled this noted Boston to a Group 2nd.

← Overleaf:

1. The well-known Can., Am., and Bda. Ch. Flo-ra's Dani Boy of Robb Isle, C.D., born July 1972, still alive, well and happy in December 1985. Top Boston Terrier in Canada, 1973 (in a tie), 1977, 1978 and 1979. Sire, Can., Am., and Eng. Ch. Apposyte Double Feature; dam, Can. Ch. Flo-ra's April Jest. Bred by Florence Gleason, British Columbia, Canada. Owned by Bob and Dianne Lowes, Wybridge, Ontario, Canada.

2. Ch. Blazermin's Mr. Mischievous, by Ch. Good Time Leroy T. Brown ex Sunwood's Black Lace, bred and owned by Lt. Col. Jim Cronen, Louisville, Kentucky.

1. Can. and Am. Ch. Ardmore's Toby Jug winning the Non-Sporting Group at Tyee K.C. on May 10, 1984. Canada's No. 3 Boston in 1980; No. 2 in 1981, and No. 1 Boston Terrier in 1983. Bred, owned, and handled by Len and Pat Read, Sidney, British Columbia, Canada.

2. Can. and Am. Ch. Agincourt Call Me Madam, handled here by Mrs. Eleanor Heit, is winning a 5-point major under judge William L. Kendrick. Agincourt Boston Terriers, Murray A. Heit, D.D.S., Milton, Ontario, Canada. This bitch is the dam of Ch. Agincourt Sweet Charity, the Top Winning Boston in Canada for 1980.

3. Am. Ch. Sumac Himself No Ka Oi, is the highest placed Boston Terrier in Alaska since the mid-1960s, consistently taking Best of Breed and Group placements. He is a son of Can. Ch. Hagerty's Royal Visitor ex Can. Ch. Hagerty's Little Rascal, was bred by Mrs. Lomer Hodge, Lennoxville, Quebec, Canada, and is owned by Charlotte M. Bilboa and Kathleen M. Searle, Alaska. No. 7 Boston Terrier in the U.S.A., Routledge Point System as of June 1985.

4. Canada's No. 1 Boston Terrier for 1982, the all-breed Best in Show winner, Can. and Am. Ch. Ardmore's Rockabye Baby, by Ch. Shebu of Kaibar ex Ardmore's Pewter Princess. Bred and owned by Len and Pat Read, Ardmore Kennels, Sidney, British Columbia, Canada.

5. Ch. Ardmore's Laird of MacKenzie, by Ch. Sherman Regards of Edclif ex Ch. Edclif's Tipperary Trixie, No. 3 Canadian Boston Terrier for 1978, bred and owned by Len and Pat Read, Sidney, British Columbia, Canada.

6. Ch. F.L.P.'s Lucky Review, by Ch. Review's Mischiefmaker ex F.L.P.'s Miss Indiana, taking a good Group placement in June 1983, completing title on the day. Owned by Bob and Dianne Lowes, Wyebridge, Ontario, Canada. Bred by F.L. Patterson, Fort Wayne, Indiana.

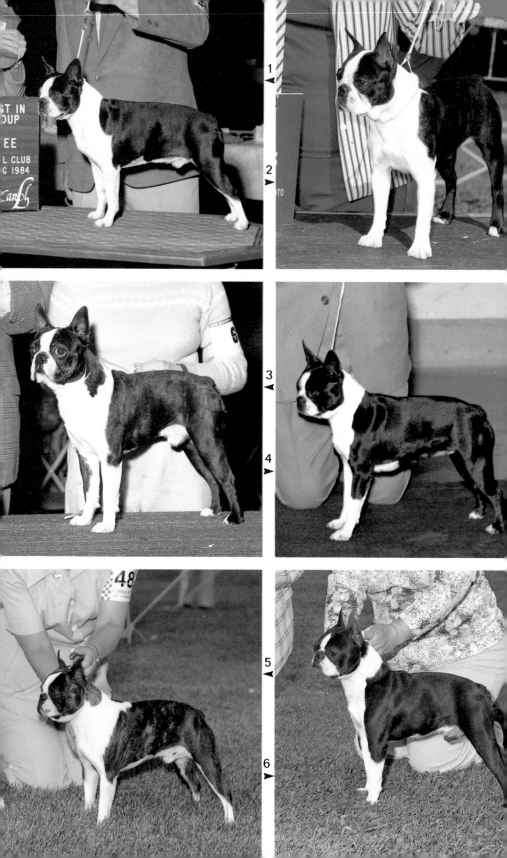

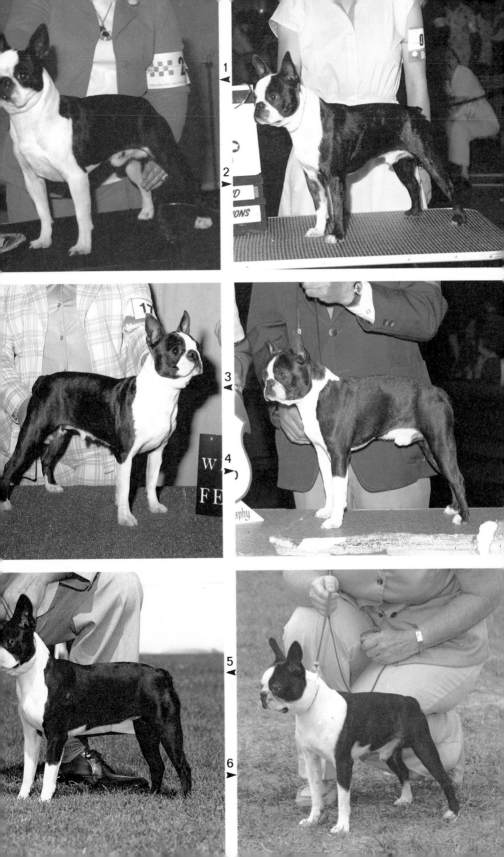

1. Can. Ch. Robb Isle Happy Son, by Ch. Dani Boy ex Ch. Ausman's Pati Cake O'Robb Isle. This Boston is also pointed in America and Bermuda. Owned by Bob and Dianne Lowes, Wyebridge, Ontario, Canada.

2. Am. and Can. Ch. Tijuana Bold as Brass, Am. and Can. C.D., was the Top Canadian Boston Terrier in 1981. Tequila Boston Terriers, Fenwick, Ontario, Canada. Pictured winning the Non-Sporting Group when just nine months old at Huronia K.C.

3. Can. Ch. Robb Isle Smylee Shannon, by Ch. Robb Isle Happy Son ex Ch. Ardell's Sugar Candy of Robb Isle is a lovely winning female owned by Bob and Dianne Lowes, Wyebridge, Ontario, Canada.

4. Can., Mex., and Am. Ch. Hayhurst's Rhett Butler, foundation stud dog at Tijuana Kennels, Fenwick, Ontario, Canada, winning an important Group placement at Seaway K.C. in 1980 for owner Terry Goss. This dog is an outstanding sire in Canada, with many champions to his credit.

5. Ch. Ardmore's Rockabye Baby at age six and a half months. By Ch. Shebu of Kaibar ex Ardmore's Pewter Princess, bred and owned by Len and Pat Read, Ardmore Boston Terriers, Sidney, British Columbia, Canada. Out of the classes at six months and two days an undefeated champion!

6. Can. Ch. Hagerty's Royal Visitor, at age nine months, taking Best Puppy in the Non-Sporting Group at Barrie K.C. in 1981. Since then (his first ring appearance), he has repeated the Best Puppy victory, gained Best of Breed 18 times and Best of Opposite Sex on nine occasions. Bred by Mrs. G.A. Hodgins, Hamilton, Ontario, he is owned by Mrs. Lomer Hodge, Lennoxville, Quebec, Canada.

1. Ch. What's Up Tiger Lily looks to be asking "what's up?" in this picture. Best of Breed and Group placing bitch owned by her breeder, Judy Griffith, and Maxine Uzoff, Houston, Texas.

2. Ch. R.T.'s Cricket of Tru-Mark, C.D. is owned by Dorothy Truman, Rockbridge Baths, Virginia.

3. Miss Janie of Bar None, U.D., owned, trained, and handled by Robert L. Breum. Highest scoring obedience Boston Terrier in the United States over a two-year period, 1967 and 1968.

4. Ch. F.L.P.'s Review was used by Carol Nooney as the model for a sketch to be used on note paper. "Billy" owned by Bob and Dianne Lowes, Wyebridge, Ontario, Canada.

1 ◄

2 ◄

3 ◄

4 ◄

← **Overleaf:**

A very promising litter of puppies at Maestro Bostons, Willie Mae and Julius "Jay" Martell, Topeka, Kansas.

1. Ch. Alexander's Dashing Dotsie by Ch. Alexander's Rose Royce ex Alexander's Polka Dot took six Bests of Breed from the classes while gaining her championship. Owned by the Alexanders, Waynesboro, Georgia.

2. Michael Wolf with Ch. Jeffords Abigail, co-owned with Mrs. Walter Jeffords during her show career; now owned by Mr. Wolf, Oxford, Pennsylvania. A multi-Best in Show (all-breed) winner with a great many Specialty and Group awards to her credit, she is here gaining Best in Show at Old Dominion in April 1978.

3. The happy winners. Ch. Staley's El-Bo's Showman with proud co-owner Michael Staley after winning their first Best in Show, all breeds, at the Cincinnati Kennel Club on May 27, 1984.

4. Ch. Yoki-En's Miss Night-N-Gale in January 1985 winning Best of Breed when only age six and a half months at Greater Clark County K.C. This homebred daughter of Ch. El-Bo's Rudy is a Dandy ex Standup-N-Cheer is, like her dam, a homebred owned by Mary and Alice Ochiai, Glendale, California.

1 ◄

2 ►

3 ◄

4 ◄

← **Overleaf:**

1. Am. and Can. Ch. Dan Jee's I'm Suzi Too winning one of her numerous Group placements, this time at Wachuset in 1980, owner-handled by Honore Rosen, Park Ridge, New Jersey.

2. Ch. Talone's Tried-N-True, Winners Dog and Best of Winners, Birmingham Specialty, November 1978. Handled by David Bolus for owners, John and Nancy Talone, Knoxville, Tennessee. Tried-N-True is by Ch. Byron's TNT ex Ch. Talone's Topper-N-Tina.

3. Regal Legacy Virginia Jazz Kid taking Winners Dog in June 1985 handled by Jon Woodward for owners, Anthony A. Antolics and Jose F. Negron, Annandale, Virginia.

4. Ch. Country Kin Scotland Yard Ace, by Ch. B.B.'s Dude's Little Hobo ex Country Kin Auntie Mame, taking Best of Winners and Best of Opposite Sex, at North Shore K.C. in 1981. Owner-handled by Mrs. Rosen, Park Ridge, New Jersey.

5. Ch. Chahary Angel of Jovan, owned by Helen Skibe, handled by breeder Ira Smoluchowski, Chahary Kennels, Rockford, Illinois. Angel is by Am. and Can. Ch. Chahary Adonis Jovan ex Ch. Chahary Beau Kay Mireille, and is pictured winning a Group placement.

6. Ch. Blazermin's Nicole of Sunwood going Best of Winners on way to the title. Owner-handled by Jim Cronen II, this dog is by Ch. Alexander Star Reward ex Top's Again Mimmie.

7. Ch. Country Kin Carmelina winning a Group 2nd at Hockamock K.C. under judge Alexander Schwartz in 1981; owner-handled by Honore Rosen. A top contender under the rating systems over several years, this lovely bitch has many Group wins and placements, along with Specialty Bests of Breed to her credit.

8. Ch. Blazermin's Family Tradition going Best of Winners. She is a daughter of Ch. Zodiac Special Beau ex Ch. Sunwood's Sweet Tradition. Owner-handled by Jim Cronen.

1. Ch. Albelarm Rather Special winning the Non-Sporting Group in 1982. Handled by co-owner Michael Wolf for himself and Mrs. Alan Robson.

2. Ch. Sunwood's Sweet Tradition, by Ch. Good Time Leroy T. Brown ex Sunwood's Crazy Daisy, taking a five-point major en route to the title, Evansville, March 1983. Handled by Jim Cronen, Louisville, Kentucky, for himself and Jill Ritchey.

3. Ch. Maestro's Blossom Dearie, by Ch. Showmans Finales Good News ex Maestro's Sonata By Reporter, pictured on the way to the title. Owned by Willie Mae and Julius "Jay" Martell, Maestro Boston Terriers, Topeka, Kansas.

4. Ch. Chappie's Little Sweetheart taking Best of Opposite Sex from the author a few years back.

5. Ch. Regal Legacy Mass Appeal by Royal Legacy Lord Marksman ex Dee Dee's Little Queen, winning the second of back-to-back five-point majors on the same weekend. Bred and owned by Jose F. Negron and Anthony A. Antolics, Regal Legacy Boston Terriers, Annandale, Virginia.

6. Ch. Mindy Mite of Little Acres by Ch. Alexander's Star Reward ex Stoney Creek's Good Bye Girl going Best of Winners en route to the title. Owner-handled by Pat and Jim Cronen, Blazermin Bostons, Louisville, Kentucky.

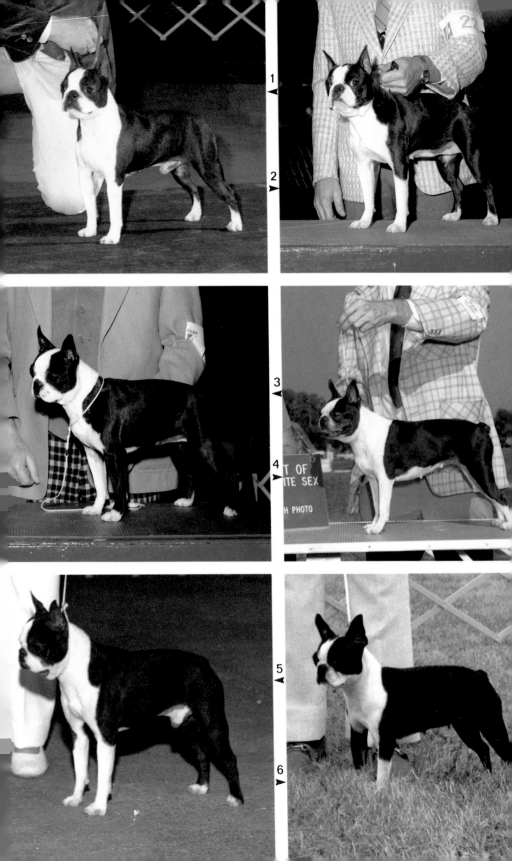

← Overleaf:

1. Ch. Country Kin Carmelina gaining a Group 2nd award at Twin Brooks K.C. in 1982. Owner-handled by Mrs. Honore Rosen.

2. Ch. Sir Whiff-N-Poof, owner-handled homebred taking Best of Breed at Santa Monica, California, May 1985. Mary K. and Alice S. Ochiai, Yoki-En Bostons, Glendale, California.

3. Allen's Wee Bonnie Bairn taking Best of Breed at Newton K.C. in 1978. Owner-handler, Mrs. L. Bettencourt.

4. Ch. Colonel Yankee Ingenuity, by Ch. El-Hi N Star Q Colonel Butono ex Austin's Adorable Ann-E winning Best of Breed at Union County in May 1983. Owned by Stephanie Barry, Miss B's Bostons.

5. Ch. Alexander's Tony taking Best of Winners at the Alabama Specialty in 1983 by Ch. Zodiac Special Beau ex Alexander's Polka Dot. Finished title with ease. Owned by the Alexanders, Waynesboro, Georgia.

6. The very famous bitch Ch. Milady Deacon of Boston, by Ch. Good Time Jody T. Brown ex Good Time Teddy J. Brown, here winning an all-breed Best in Show. Handled by Jerry Rigden for owners, Dr. and Mrs. Robert Ritchey, Canal Fulton, Ohio. Bred by Thomas L. Enwright.

Overleaf: →

1. Ch. Regal Legacy Razzle Dazzle, by Ch. Regal Legacy First Edition ex Ch. Regal Legacy No Finah Dinah, a homebred owned by Jose F. Negron and Anthony A. Antolics, Regal Legacy, Annandale, Virginia. Pictured completing title at Hunterdon Hills K.C. in 1985.

2. Am. and Can. Ch. Sunwoods Bit of Brandy taking points towards her title in 1984. Owned by Mrs. Anita G. Ciannilli, Cia's Boston Terriers, Syracuse, New York.

3. Ch. Robb Isle X-Caliber, by Robb Isle Timber ex Robb Isle Sasha, born October 16, 1984, pictured finishing Canadian championship at age nine and a half months, at which same show she was third in the Non-Sporting Group, first in Puppy Group, and Best Puppy in Show. Now co-owned and handled by Lorna Lowes, Wyebridge, Ontario, Canada and has numerous Group wins and placements.

4. Standup-N-Cheer going from Winners Bitch to Best of Winners and Best of Opposite Sex, owner-handled, at K.C. of Riverside in 1981. Mary K. and Alice S. Ochiai, Yoki-En Bostons, Glendale, California.

5. Am. and Can. Ch. Clasen's Campus Kid, the first Boston Terrier and the first champion owned by Marc and Honore Rosen, Scotland Yard Kennels, Park Ridge, New Jersey. Here taking Winners Dog at the Boston Terrier Club of Miami, Florida, Specialty, January 1975.

6. Ch. Regal Legacy First Edition, by Am. and Can. Ch. Simms Hi Hope Mr. Hobo ex Regal Legacy Elenora Hyregards. Handled by Patricia Johnson for owners Anthony A. Antolics and Jose F. Negron, Annandale, Virginia. Pictured taking Winners Dog at Oak Ridge in 1983.

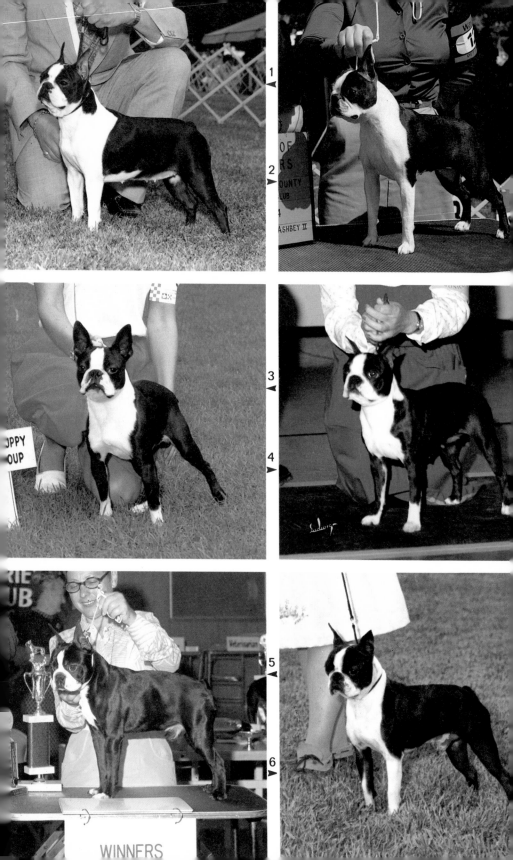

1

2

3

4

5

6

← Overleaf:

1. Ch. Jeffords Scotland Yard Beau, by Ch. Jeffords Minute Man ex Jeffords Scotland Yard Lady, owner-handled by Honore Rosen, Park Ridge, New Jersey, to Winners, Best of Winners, and Best of Opposite Sex at Westchester K.C. in 1981.

2. Ch. Blazermin's Waltzing Matilda going Best of Breed, owner-handled by Pat Cronen. By Ch. Leroy T. Brown ex Sunwood's Black Lace.

3. Eight weeks old here, this pensive puppy grew up to become Ch. Country Kin Scotland Yard Ace, Marc and Honore Rosen, owners, Park Ridge, New Jersey.

4. Am., Can., and Bda. Ch. Hayhurst's Rhett Butler owned by Terry Goss, Fenwick, Ontario, Canada.

5. Ch. Maestro's Billy Whiz Bang, a grandson of Ch. Zodiac's Special Beau, as usual owner-handled by Robert L. Breum. Pictured winning the Boston Terrier Club of Topeka Specialty Show in 1985.

6. This beautifully matched and very outstanding Boston Terrier brace consists of Ch. Regal Legacy Sorceress Spell and Ch. Regal Legacy Cisco The Kid, both sired by Am. and Can. Ch. Simms Hihope Mr. Hobo. Handled by Anthony A. Antolics for himself and co-breeder/owner Jose F. Negron, Regal Legacy Kennels, Annandale, Virginia. Here winning Best Non-Sporting Brace at Carroll Kennel Club in 1984.

Overleaf: →

1. Ch. Regal Legacy Sorceress Spell, by Am. and Can. Ch. Mr. Simms Hi-hope Mr. Hobo ex Command's Dancing Tamara was bred by Anthony A. Antolics and Jose F. Negron, Annandale, Virginia. Owner-handled by Mr. Antolics pictured here.

2. Ch. Sir Whiff-N-Poof taking Group 4th at Sir Francis Drake K.C. in April 1984. Handled by Michael J. Dougherty for owners and breeders, Mary and Alice Ochiai, Glendale, California.

3. Ch. El-Bo's Rudy Is A Dandy receiving his Group award from the arms of Bob Candland, co-breeder, owner, and handler.

4. This lovely photo of Honore Rosen with Am. and Can. Ch. Dan Jee's I'm Suzi Too, Group winner owned by Mr. and Mrs. Marc Rosen, Park Ridge, New Jersey, appeared on the back cover of the June 1980 issue of *Kennel Review,* and is an Alton Anderson photograph.

FIRST PRIZE
SOUTH BAY
KENNEL CLUB

← **Overleaf:**

1. Am. and Can. Ch. Dan Jee's I'm Suzi Too, by Ch. Toby Junior II ex Ch. Clasen's Sweet Sue, was No. 1 Boston Terrier bitch for 1980 and No. 3 overall in the breed. Owned by Marc and Honore Rosen, Scotland Yard Boston Terriers, Park Ridge, New Jersey.

2. Ch. Sunwoods Merrie Munchin by Ch. Nez Pousse's Wright Choice ex Stoney Creeks D A Tinkerbell, is one of the many outstanding homebreds owned by Dr. and Mrs. Robert Ritchey at Canal Fulton, Ohio. Winning Best of Breed and a Group placement at Beaver County K.C. in 1981, Jerry Rigden handling.

3. An intent Rudy is watching that snack coming to him from Bob's fingers, now that the Group is "over and won." Ch. El-Bo's Rudy Is A Dandy with co-breeder/owner and handler Bob Candland.

4. Ch. Blazermin's Valentine taking points towards the title owner-handled by Jim Cronen II, Louisville, Kentucky. Sired by Ch. Blazer of Top's Again ex Ch. Mindy Mite.

Overleaf: →

1. Best in Show winner Ch. Jeffords Constance taking Best of Breed at Westminster 1980.

2. Ch. Sunwoods Star Attraction, by Ch. Alexander's Star Reward ex Sunwoods Lady Dyanna, bred and owned by Dr. and Mrs. Robert Ritchey, Canal Fulton, Ohio. Here taking Best of Breed at Trumbull in 1984, Jerry Rigden handling.

3. Ch. Schubo's Roamin' Romancer, a Group winner from the Puppy Class, was bred by Wes and Karen Schultz, sired by Ch. Schubo's Travelin' Romancer ex Schubo's Misty Moon. Handled by Wes Schultz. Now owned by Jill Ritchey in Ohio.

4. Ch. Showman's Finale Good News, bred/owned/handled by Russell F. Dowell, Kansas City, Missouri, represents the noted Showman bloodline, being by Ch. Reporter's Finale ex Showman's Sassy Babe. This handsome dog is the fifth generation on his dam's side. He is owned by Mr. Dowell. Although never specialed, Good News has Best of Breed wins to his credit, including one occasion on which he gained the top award by defeating 14 champions in the specials class. He is proving an outstanding young sire, his progeny including Ch. Maestro's Billy Whiz Bang, Ch. Maestro's Koul Kio Miff, Ch. Hi Crest Bonnie Annie Laurie, Ch. Showman's Jolly St. Nick, Ch. Maestro's Blossom Dearie, Ch. Showman's Holiday Noel, and a number of others who should be finished by now.

5. Best in Show, all-breeds, at the Cincinnati K.C., May 1984. Ch. Staley's El-Bo's Showman, owned by Michael and Beverly Staley, Edgewood, Kentucky. The judge was Mrs. Walton.

6. Ch. Sunwoods Classic Design, by Ch. Mike Mar's Truly Special ex Ch. Sunwoods Sweet Tradition, winning the breed at K.C. of Yorkville, Illinois, for breeders/owners Jill Ritchey and Jim Cronen.

← Overleaf:

1. Ch. Sunwoods Rearding Star, by Ch. Alexander Star Reward ex Sunwoods Cupie Doll, taking points in 1985. Elaine Rigden handling for breeders/owners Dr. and Mrs. Robert Ritchey, Canal Fulton, Ohio.

2. Ch. Edclif's Mai Janii of Ardmore, by Ch. Sherman Regards of Edclif ex Tipperary Bambi, Canada's No. 2 Boston Terrier for 1977. Bred and owned by Len and Pat Reed, Ardmore Boston Terriers, Sidney, British Columbia, Canada.

3. Ch. Jeffords Constance following her Best in Show win at Western Pennsylvania over 2,000 dogs in 1979. Originally owned by Mrs. Walter M. Jeffords and Mr. Michael Wolf, Constance, whose show honors include, in addition to many Specialty and Group wins and all-breed Bests in Show, Best of Breed at Westminster in 1980, is now co-owned by Mr. Wolf with Mrs. Alan Robson.

4. The A.K.C. Centennial Dog Show had as its Best of Breed Boston Terrier Ch. Staley's El-Bo's Showman, owned by Michael and Beverly Staley, Edgewood, Kentucky. The judge, Emil Klinckhardt.

5. Ch. Regal Legacy Anthony Ringlord, by Ch. Brandywine's Gusty Specialty ex Rip's Penny Lane. Owned by Anthony A. Antolics, co-breeder with Jose F. Negron. Pictured as a puppy completing title at Forsyth K.C. November 1982 judged by the author.

6. The incomparable Ch. Zodiac's Special Beau, owned and handled by Robert L. Breum, Omaha, Nebraska, taking a Group 1st. This magnificent Boston Terrier had to his credit ten all-breed Bests in Show, nine Boston Terrier Specialty Bests of Breed, 38 Group firsts—and is the sire of 38 champions to date! What more can we say?

1. Am. and Can. Ch. Simms Hihope Mr. Hobo, sire of 11 champions. Mr. Hobo is a son of Am. and Can. Ch. Simms Hihopes Mr. Chips ex Clasen's Hy-Tone Baby. Bred by Margaret M. Simms. Owned by Anthony A. Antolics and Jose F. Negron, Annandale, Virginia.

2. Future "stars" in the Boston Terrier world, these lovely babies were bred at Maestro, Willie Mae and Julius "Jay" Martell, Topeka, Kansas.

3. Ch. What's Up Tiger Lily, for two years in the Top Ten, by Can. and Am. Ch. Kimkev's Sundance Kid ex Apollo's Flashing Fancy. Bred by Judy Griffith, co-owner with Maxine Uzoff, Houston, Texas.

4. Ch. Country Kin Carmelina, consistent Group and Specialty winner, pictured at Naugatuck Valley in 1981. Owned and handled by Mrs. Honore Rosen, Scotland Yard Kennels, Park Ridge, New Jersey. No. 2 Bitch, No. 5 Boston Terrier for 1981; No. 7 Boston Terrier 1982 and 1983; No. 1 Bitch, owner-handled, those two years; and No. 11 Boston for 1984. A bitch of quality.

5. At eight weeks old, future Ch. Jeffords Scotland Yard Beau already is showing the promise that led to his completing title at just seven months and two days! In the arms of his owner here, Mrs. Honore Rosen, Park Ridge, New Jersey.

6. Ch. Alexander's Country Sunshine, by Ch. Zodiac Special Beau ex Alexander's Polka Dot, was Best of Breed at the Birmingham Specialty in 1984. Owned by Jim and Linda Alexander, Waynesboro, Georgia.

1 ▶

2 ▶

3 ▶

4 ▶

5 ▶

6 ▶

← Overleaf:

1. Ch. Blazermin's Nicole of Sunwoods going Best of Winners, owner-handled by Jim Cronen, Louisville, Kentucky. By Ch. Alexander Star Reward ex Top's Again Minnie.

2. The magnificent bitch, Ch. Jefford's Abigail, made Boston Terrier history with wins such as this one. Best in Show at Kennel Club of Philadelphia in 1977, under the co-ownership of Mrs. Walter M. Jeffords and Michael Wolf, who is handling.

3. Ch. Clasen's Mr. Chips, by Ch. Toby Junior II ex Shani Wynter Brooke, owned by Mrs. Harry N. Clasen, Mechanicville, New York. Completed title in 1974.

4. Ch. Regal Legacy No Finah Dinah, by Am. and Can. Ch. Simm's Hihope Mr. Hobo ex Decorous Dinah. A homebred owned by Jose F. Negron and Anthony A. Antolics. Pictured taking Winners Bitch at the Boston Terrier Club of Greater Cincinnati, May 1982, over a class entry of 42 bitches, the largest entry at a Boston Terrier Club Show in 33 years.

5. Ch. Milady Deacon of Boston taking Best in Show. Handled by Jerry Rigden for Dr. and Mrs. Robert Ritchey, Canal Fulton, Ohio. Bred by Thomas L. Enwright, Milady is a daughter of Ch. Good Time Jody T. Brown ex Good Time Teddy J. Brown.

6. In the Best in Show circle, as on so many occasions, Ch. El-Bo's Rudy Is A Dandy shows off all his excellence as he stands with Bob Candland through trophy presentation. Bred, owned, and handled by Eleanor and Bob Candland, Lake Elsinore, California.

Overleaf: →

1. Play time. Ch. Talone's Ruff-N-Tuff *(right)* with his sire, Ch. Talone's Tried and True. Owned by John and Nancy Talone, Knoxville, Tennessee.

2. Puppies from Tijuana Kennels, Fenwick, Ontario, Canada.

3. Can. Ch. Tijuana's Tequila Sunrise with litter sired by Am. and Can. Ch. Tijuana's Bold as Brass, C.D. Tijuana Bostons, Fenwick, Ontario, Canada.

4. Ch. Talone's Anniversary Girl, the first homebred champion owned by John and Nancy Talone, Knoxville, Tennessee, is of Iowana and Showman breeding, sired by Hilton's Little Sparky Boy ex Talone's Tippy Toes.

5. Honore Rosen with "Beau," age six weeks.

6. Ch. Kingway Prelude, by Ch. Iowana's Sundancer ex Ken Lee's Dealers Fancy Noel, finished title in 1985. Bred and owned by Leonard L. Myers, Kingway Bostons, Denver, Colorado.

1 ►
2 ►
3 ►
4 ►
5 ►
6 ►

1

2

3

4

5

6

7

8

← **Overleaf:**

1. Don't you want a Boston puppy right this minute??? These are owned by Dorothy Truman, Rockbridge Baths, Virginia.

2. These baby Bostons are just four weeks old. By Bold As Brass from Tequila Sunrise, they are owned by Terry Goss, Fenwick, Ontario, Canada.

3. These two young Boston charmers are now Ch. Sunwoods Lookin Good and Sunwoods Poppin Fresh. Both sired by Ch. Alexander's Star Reward and breeder-owned by Dr. and Mrs. Robert Ritchey, Canal Fulton, Ohio.

4. Bostons get on well with other breeds, of which this one's owner, Mrs. Ira Smoluchowski, Rockford, Illinois, has several. Here Chahary Amie is with a Brussels Griffon friend.

5. Ch. Edclif's Mai Janii of Ardmore, the old professional, waiting to go into the ring with her six-month-old nervous buddy who is now Ch. Ardmore's Laird of Dundee, homebred and also owned by Len and Pat Read, Ardmore Boston Terriers, Sidney, British Columbia, Canada.

6. Am. and Can. Ch. Kimkev's Sundance Kid, by Ch. Kimkev's Country Gentleman ex Kimkev's Scarlet. This beautiful and typey little dog was on the Top Ten list for two years and has some excellent wins to his credit. Breeder, Betty Swick. Owner, Peggy Clark, M.D., Albuquerque, New Mexico. Handled by Judy Webb. Photo courtesy of Maxine Uzoff.

7. Game time! Two of the champions at Chahary Kennels each seeking possession of the toy. Mrs. Ira Smoluchowski, owner, Rockford, Illinois.

8. The dam in this photo is Ch. Bar None's Fayme. The sire of the puppies, not pictured, is Ch. Sabe's Lucky Punch. The puppies, all bitches, from *left* to *right* grew up to become Ch. Bar None's Elegance, owned by Janet and Dick Rees; Bar None's Mademoiselle, owned by Kathy Brey; Ch. Bar None's Classic, owned by John and Marby Kelly; and Ch. Bar None's Vogue, owned by Linda Alexander. Ch. Bar None's Fayme is a daughter of Ch. Zodiac's Special Beau. She is owned by, and the pups were bred by, Robert L. Breum and G.R. Decker.

Overleaf: →

A basket of Christmas cheer! Regal Legacy Boston puppies by Regal Legacy Lord Marksman ex Regal Legacy That Girl Marlo, exemplifying consistency through line-breeding. Bred by Anthony A. Antolics and Jose F. Negron, Regal Legacy, Annandale, Virginia.

159

Chapter 4

Canadian Kennel Stories

The people of Boston, where the breed was originated and developed, take a very special pride in Boston Terriers, as well they might. It is not too great a distance from the Boston area of Massachusetts to Canada; and it did not really take Canadian dog fanciers any time at all to learn of the new breed and promptly become intrigued with it.

During the 1920's, Boston Terriers fairly skyrocketed in increasing numbers of American Kennel Club registrations and dog show entries.

Their popularity seemed boundless. The same condition existed to our north in the Canadian Kennel Club. Both places were moving right along with the breed, and from then on Boston Terriers from both of these countries have been gaining American-Canadian Championships on their dogs, which in those days were considered to be International Championships, as they meant championships in more than just one country. As some were bred in Canada, others in the United States, it is evident the the correct type and quality was being produced by breeders in both places, making their dogs competitive and creating excitement and satisfaction for the winners.

Boston Terrier activity in Canada was not limited to any few areas. Rather it is countrywide as you will note from the kennel stories. The Boston Terrier Club of Canada is centrally located in the Manitoba area, with officers in Winnipeg and Brandon. One of their great services to the breed is their publication of the outstanding monthly newsletter, *The Boston Snorter*, circulated free to the membership. James Shawara is President; Ms. Sharon Davis and Mr. and Mrs. Les H. Munroe Treasurer and Newsletter editors respectively.

AGINCOURT

Agincourt Boston Terriers at Milton, Ontario, Canada, are owned by Murray A. Heit, D.D.S., who has for some eighteen years been breeding Boston Terriers, with Beagles as the "odd breed" from time to time.

The Heits own the very famous bitch, American and Canadian Champion Agincourt Sweet Charity, who has been recognized as No. 1 Boston Bitch in Canada and who has the distinction of being a Best in Show winner. She completed her American Championship at the Detroit Specialty. She is the particular pride of her breeder owner, which is certainly understandable considering her quality and her success.

American and Canadian Champion Heit's Dusty Wee Dodie, daughter of American and Canadian Champion Chappie's Little Stardust ex Terrylea Sue Coquette, finished in 1975 for Dr. Heit, doing so with a prestigious record. This superb bitch won her first "major" under the late Alva Rosenberg, also gaining points from the late Vincent Perry and from the author. She has produced champions and has champion grandchildren, a bitch who has contributed well to her breed and to Agincourt.

American and Canadian Champion Royal Yorks Duke of Agincourt was No. 1 Boston Terrier in Canada in 1976. Charity No. 1 in 1980, and Angie, Charity's puppy, was No. 1 Bitch in 1984.

Nowadays Dr. Heit limits his exhibiting activities in favor of judging, as he is now doing several Groups.

We must pay our respects, when writing of Agincourt, to the beautiful bitch who is Charity's dam. She is Canadian and American Champion Agincourt Call Me Honey, whose contribution has been considerable.

Can. and Am. Ch. Agincourt Sweet Charity, 1980's Top Canadian Boston Terrier, bred and owned by Murray A. Heit, D.D.S., Milton, Ontario.

Can. and Am. Ch. Ardmore's Toby Jug, Canada's No. I Boston Terrier for 1983, bred, owned, and handled by Len and Pat Read, Ardmore Boston Terriers, Sidney, British Columbia.

Can. Ch. Robb Isle Happy Son, by Ch. Flora's Dani Boy of Robb Isle, C.D. ex Ch. Ausman's Pati Cake of Robb Isle, C.D. Owned by Bob and Dianne Lowes, Wyebridge, Ontario.

Left: Ch. Shy Susie Que, by Clements Bim Beau ex Clements Tammy Tee, was No. 12 Boston Terrier in Canada for the year 1980. Owned by Ruth K. Chapman, Thunder Bay, Ontario. *Right:* Can. Ch. Flora's Dani Boy of Robb Isle, C.D. winning one of his Group 1sts for owners Bob and Dianne Lowes, Wyebridge, Ontario.

ARDMORE

Ardmore Kennels has been a registered company, within the "Companies Act," and a member in good standing of the Canadian Kennel Club since the mid-1970's. The owners, Len and Pat Read at Sidney, British Columbia, Canada, concentrate on only one breed, Boston Terriers.

A husband and wife team, the Reads handle, train and show all of their own dogs. They started 15 years ago with just one very good Boston bitch, and through selective linebreeding, have built up their kennel to three champion stud dogs and ten or twelve very nice and carefully bred brood bitches.

All Ardmore Bostons are sold with a written statement that the puppy is healthy, and these breeders stand behind this guarantee fully. Although kenneled, all Ardmore Bostons are rotated in pairs as house dogs. Therefore they are socialized and all are house-trained pets.

The Reads show their own Bostons both in Canada and in the United States, and some of theirs have been among the Top Ten Canadian Bostons for over ten years. Over the past few years their Bostons have ranked in the Top Three Canadian Bostons. These honors are accounted for by Champion Edclif's Mai Janii of Ardmore, Champion Ardmore's Laird of MacKenzie, Canadian and American Champion Ardmore's Toby Jug, and Canadian and American Champion Ardmore's Rockabye Baby.

The Reads have also trained their Boston Terriers in obedience, and are presently working on a C.D.X. on their second obedience dog.

Ardmore Kennels are devoted to careful linebreeding, good temperament and conformation—happy, healthy, well-adjusted dogs.

ROBB ISLE

Robb Isle Boston Terriers, at Wyebridge, Ontario, are owned by Bob and Dianne Lowes who, in 1965, went out to purchase their first purebred dog, a German Shepherd female. The following year it was decided to find a stud for her; but that was not enough—they decided to purchase the dog, too. Thus Robb Isle Kennels was born and registered in 1966.

It was in June 1971 that the Lowes bought their first Boston Terrier, who became Champion Miss Pickles of Robb Isle. Then came Champion Ardell's Sugar Candy of Robb Isle. With these two excellent females, obviously the Lowes needed an outstanding stud dog. Following many letters and much discussion and thought, Dani Boy joined the family, later to become Canadian, American and Bermudian Champion Flo-ra's Dani Boy, C.D. (the latter thrown in "just for fun"), who was bred by Florence Gleason in British Columbia. Dani Boy was sired by English, Canadian, and American Champion Apposyte Double Feature ex Canadian Champion Flo-ra's April Jest, and he made history by becoming the Top Boston Terrier (a tie that year) in 1973. This was followed by Top Boston for him in 1977, 1978 and 1979. His Canadian show ring successes included four Group firsts and 38 additional Group placements from 172 times Best of Breed.

In the United States, Dani Boy gained his title with four majors, including a 5-point Best of Winners at the Cincinnati Specialty. In Bermuda, he took five majors; five Bests of Breed; and two Group thirds, completing his title there in 1978.

Dani Boy was born July 26, 1972. Dianne Lowes comments, "he has gotten a little more gray, but still loves his meals on time. Also he still looks for the girls, although I don't think he would know what to do with them now."

The Lowes have made a record with their Bostons which is very outstanding. Among the winners they have either bred or owned are Champion Flo-ra's Lady Jennifer, Champion Tops Again Tina of Robb Isle, Champion Flo-ra's Joyful Miss, Champion Ausman's Pati Cake O'Robb Hill, Champion Robb Isle Happy Son, Champion Supreme Hell of Robb Isle, Champion Schubo's Dashin' Dandy, Champion Schubo's Shimmerin' Nugget, Champion Robb Isle Smylee Shannon, Champion Van's Robb Isle Gabriel, Champion F.L.P.'s Lucky Review, Champion Robb Isle Whispering Hope, Champion Flo-ra's Miss Penny Ante, Champion Clown's Echo of Escort, Champion Robb Isle Re-Echo, Champion Flo-ra's Ding A Ling Doll, Champion King's Tyrus Bully, Champion Sonny's Robb Isle Yonge Brave, Champion Robb Isle Danielle of Mardon, Champion Sonny's Robb Isle Yank, Champion Robb Isle Flashy Belle Starr, Champion Robb Isle Olee Bear, Champion Robb Isle X-Caliber, and with points, Robb Isle Northern Performance.

Family portrait, and champions all, at Robb Isle Bostons, owned by Bob and Dianne Lowes, Wyebridge, Ontario. *Left to right:* Tina, Sonny, Nugget, Andy, Miss Pickle, Shannon, Joy, Dolly,and Dani Boy.

Can. Ch. Hayhurst's Southern Belle *(left),* by Ch. Hayhurst Morgan's Finale ex Ch. Hayhurst's Best of Show Biz; and Can. Ch. Sumac's Short Stuff *(right),* by Can. Ch. Harmony's Tough Stuff Sumac ex Can. Ch. Hayhurst's Southern Bell. Both owned by Mrs. Lomer Hodge, who is the breeder, as well, of Short Stuff. Southern Belle was bred by John M. White, the son of Myrtle Hayhurst who started with Bostons in the 1930's. Mrs. Hodge tells us, when John died, he had represented 43 generations of Mrs. Hayhurst's direct line breeding, Southern Belle being one of the last Hayhurst Bostons in Canada now. Short Stuff age 9 months, pictured here upon completion, of his championship. He is now at stud in a Vermont kennel.

Dianne adds, as a "p.s." to the above, "Somewhere in there we ourselves had four girls who are all champions. But they are human "pups." And we have three granddaughters now who look like real winners, too." It is easy to see that the years have been busy ones for this family!

Dani Boy sired ten champions (to his owners' knowledge).

The current young "star" at this kennel is Canadian Champion Robb Isle X-Caliber, by Robb Isle Timber from Robb Isle Sasha who was born in October 1984. This splendid youngster finished at age 9 1/2 months in six shows with Group third, Best in Puppy Group, and Best Puppy in Show. Then before becoming a full year old, over one weekend he took a Group first, a Group second, and a Group third and two Best in Puppy Groups. He is now starting out as a stud. X-Caliber is co-owned by Bob and Dianne Lowes with their daughter Lorna Lowes.

RUJAY

Rujay Boston Terriers belong to Ruth K. Chapman at Thunder Bay, Ontario, Canada, where the grand matriarch of the kennel is the lovely bitch Champion Shy Susie Que.

Susie, who is by Clements Bim Beau ex Clements Tammy Tee, is linebred from mostly Truitt and Currie stock. Susie was first shown at a three day event, July 25 through 27, in 1980. On her first day, she went Best of Winners, Best of Breed, Best Puppy in breed and Group, and third in the Non-Sporting Group under judge R. William Taylor.

Again shown in September 1980 at another three day event, she also fared well; by the end of the year she had become No. 2 Boston Terrier in Canada.

Early in 1981, Susie raised a litter of five puppies, then returned to the show ring to complete her championship, which she did on her second day of showing as a now mature bitch. Then she retired permanently to raise puppies, which she does so well.

Susie is the dam of 31 handsome Bostons, all free whelped. Many have followed in her paw-prints, re-affirming her quality and good looks.

A son of Susie's, Champion Rujay's Super Jet, owned by Loretta Martin, became Canada's No. 3 Boston for 1984 with very limited showing. He is sired by Handee's Jet Special. A daughter, Champion Rujay's Bonnie Sue, gained title easily within one year of showing. Bonnie is a daughter, as well, of Syringas Victory Tuxedo Man from the United States, and is the dam of Rujay's Bonnie Cindy Sue, who is just starting her show career. And so Susie's grand-pups are also carrying on in the family tradition.

Susie is just past five years of age and, to quote her owner, "acts and looks just like a pup." It is hoped to have more puppies from her to join the winners she has already produced and their offspring.

SUMAC

Sumac Boston Terriers have been active since 1969, when they were founded by Lomer and Dorene Hodge. It was not until ten years later however, that these fanciers from Lennoxville, Quebec, started to show their dogs; and then they took a puppy just for practice. When this puppy returned home having won Best of Breed over an entry of eight Bostons, then Best Puppy in Group, her owners had been fully converted to the role of exhibitors.

Can. Ch. Hagerty's Little Rascal, by Can. Ch. J.D., Grand Command ex Can. Ch. Hagerty's Evening Sunset, bred by Mrs. G.A. Hodgins. This famous dog owned by Mrs. Lomer Hodge, Lennoxville, Quebec is a multiple Best of Opposite Sex, Best of Breed, and Group placement winner.

Since then the Hodges have finished at least one champion yearly, two on some occasions, except for the year during which they campaigned Champion Hagerty's Little Rascal as a special, concentrating on just this one over that period. Despite limited travel and showing, Rascal completed the year in 1983's Top Five, which was nice going indeed.

Sumac is a small kennel, averaging six to eight bitches plus two stud dogs. Dorene feels this is enough to care for properly and do the dogs full justice. Her breeding program, also, is limited. If they have free whelpers, they breed such a bitch twice, then skip the third season. Her top producing bitches are from Hayhurst-Hagerty and Harmony-Clasen bloodlines. Mrs. Hodge has been able to trace most of their pedigrees back to 1900.

Mrs. Hodge comments that at first they outcrossed entirely in their breeding plans. But wanting to improve the breed, they decided to buy top quality stock and concentrate on linebreeding, which has worked out well for them in the production of some truly lovely Bostons

Mrs. Hodge is keenly on the alert and deeply concerned over the prevalence of eye problems in Bostons, especially the existence of juvenile cataracts. She notes that there are several breeders in Canada, including herself, who are test breeding in an effort to eliminate any lines producing blind puppies. She herself has studied the genetics of the problem, and is encouraging others to do likewise. I am sure that she would be delighted to hear from anyone anxious to join in this project.

TIJUANA

Tijuana Kennels are located at Fenwick, Ontario, and this kennel is the home of some very superior Boston Terriers who have been bred and/or owned by Terry Goss and by Judy Campbell.

The foundation stud dog here is Canadian, American and Mexican Champion Hayhurst's Rhett Butler, bred by John M. White, born March 7, 1978, owned by Terry Goss. Rhett Butler is a son of International Champion Hayhurst Morgan Finale (Hayhurst Nip and Tuck–International Champion Hayhurst Tops Again Kate) from Canadian Champion Bess of Show Man (American Champion Royale Show Man–Mione Token of Perfection). Terry says of this dog, "He has, to the best of knowledge, produced

Can. Ch. Sumac Herself Lady Ascot, puppy bitch owned by Mrs. Doreen Hodge, Lennoxville, Quebec. A homebred by Ch. Kraft's Duke of Howdee ex Sumac Herself Baby Snooks. Starting her show career at seven months, this lovely bitch completed title in four shows by age eight months, taking a Group placement and Best Puppy in Group on that same occasion, Chareauguay K.C., June 1985.

more Canadian champions during the past five years than any other Boston in Canada."

Principal current winner at Tijuana is the Rhett Butler son, Canadian and American Champion Tijuana Bold as Brass, Canadian and American C.D., who is now competing in obedience at the C.D.X. level. This dog was the No. 1 Boston in Canada in 1981, and No. 2 in 1982.

An informal snapshot of Can. Ch. Tijuana's Bold As Brass owned by Terry Goss, Fenwick, Ontario.

Can. Ch. Bold Mischief of Tijuana taking Best Puppy in Breed at Limestone K.C., 1985. Sired by Can. and Am. Ch. Tijuana's Bold as Brass, C.D. (Can., Am., and Mex. Ch. Hayhurst's Rhett Butler–Ch. Tijuana's Sweet Mischief) ex Ch. Tijuana's Tequila Sunrise (Rhett Butler-Bilhaven Tops Again Bev). Bred by Judy Campbell. Owned by Terry Goss, Fenwick, Ontario.

For the future, hopes are high for the success of Champion Bold Mischief at Tijuana, bred by Judy Campbell, born December 17, 1984. A daughter of Bold as Brass, Mischief is from Champion Tijuana Tequila Sunrise, thus a double granddaughter of Canadian, American, and Mexican Champion Hayhurst's Rhett Butler. A champion at age seven months, this superb little bitch has been widely admired for her type and her excellent action.

Chapter 5

The Boston Terrier Club of America

The Boston Terrier Club of America, American Kennel Club member, parent club for this breed, became known as such in the year 1891, although it had actually been formed two years earlier as the Bull Terrier Club of America. The club caused considerable disapproval on the part of the Bull Terrier fanciers, their claim being that these round headed dogs were not truly Bull Terriers — which, of course, was true. Referring to the breed in the Stud Book in 1893, as well as the club membership in the A.K.C., it seemed appropriate to call them "Boston" Terriers since the breed had been developed in that city.

It has been a history of progress for the Boston Terrier Club of America, which can well take pride in the handsome dogs created in the breed over the years. The Boston Terrier developed from the original Bulldogs and terriers, is a dog of great beauty; well balanced, clean cut, beautifully colored, with soft and beautiful expression and a lot of style. He truly well deserves the title by which he frequently is described — the American gentleman of the canine world.

President of the Boston Terrier Club of America at the end of 1985 is Joan Eckert of Mendon, Massachusetts. Vice-President,

Mina Lehr, Minneapolis, Minnesota. Recording Secretary, Maryann Caruso, St. Clair Shores, Michigan. Corresponding Secretary, Nancy Washburn, Orange Road, New Salem, Massachusetts, 01355; Treasurer, Ruth Lieberg, South Windsor, Connecticut. American Kennel Club Delegate, Kathleen Kelly, Fieldstone Court, Fallston, MD 21047. The Board of Directors consists of Arthur Huddleston, Northridge, California; Janet Rees, Overland Park, Kansas; Edna Swift, Beaverton, Oregon; Norman Randall, Annandale, Virginia; and Mary Alice Niebaurer, Cassopolis, Michigan.

As you will note, this represents a wide coverage of various areas in the United States. The club's headquarters are, of course, in Boston.

In addition to the parent club, there are numerous regional clubs devoted to the breed located in many areas. If you are a Boston Terrier owner with any thought in mind of breeding, showing, or working in obedience with your dog, you will find membership in at least one or two of these organizations will prove to your advantage. Most people enjoy membership in the National,

Boston Terrier Club of Maryland Specialty 1968 was won by this lovely and famous bitch, Ch. Dynamic Doll, owner-handled by Roy S. Kibler of Maine. Miss Ina Lamb, holding rosette, is the judge, herself a well-known Boston breeder.

1946 Boston Terrier Club of Detroit Specialty Show. Third from left, Vin Perry with Ch. Globe Glowing Beauty. This class is an excellent example of the very high quality Boston Terriers in competition at that period.

to keep abreast of what is taking place within their breed; and in a regional club for participation in nearby activities. Most clubs nowadays provide not just an annual Specialty Show but numerous other activities as well which are helpful to the membership. These may be training classes (for obedience training and/or the teaching of show routine to you and your dog), which will go a long way to bolstering your self-confidence when you and your dog are ready to hit the competitive areas; Match Shows where your puppies can gain experience and get the feel of "in-the-ring self-assurance"; participation in meetings and club matters; attending meetings with interesting and instructive guest speakers appearing now and again to talk on matters important to you as a Boston Terrier owner, to name just a few examples.

A list of regional clubs in your area can be obtained from the American Kennel Club at 51 Madison Avenue, New York, N.Y. 10010, in return for a note or telephone call.

Ch. Staley's El-Bo's Showman. No. I Boston Terrier in both the *Canine Chronicle* and *Routledge System* ratings, is owned by Michael and Beverly Staley, Edgewood, Kentucky.

Chapter 6

Standards of the Breed

The standard of the breed, to which one hears and reads such frequent references, is the guide to those interested in breeding, showing, judging, or just becoming acquainted with a specific breed of dog. It outlines, in minute detail, each and every feature of that breed, both in physical characteristics and in temperament; it accurately describes the dog from whisker to tail, creating a clear impression of what is to be considered correct or incorrect, the features comprising "breed type" and the probable temperament and behavior pattern of typical members of that breed.

The standard is the guide for breeders endeavoring to produce dogs of quality for the show ring. It is the tool with which judges evaluate the dogs, enabling them to reach their decisions in the show ring. It draws for new fanciers a word picture of what breeders and judges are seeking, of what the features of an ideal dog should be in accordance with the requirements of his breed. It tells what is beautiful, what adds up to correct type, and what makes the dog able to fill the purposes for which the breed was developed. It is the result of many patient hours spent in study and in research and in dedicated work by fanciers with the best interests of the breed at heart.

Our present Boston Terrier standard represents the best of the earlier ones, combined occasionally with modernization or clarification to make for better understanding. It is a carefully thought out tool for the protection of the breed, and our understanding of what the words are telling us is essential for our true appreciation of quality Boston Terriers.

Earlier Boston Terrier fanciers had a big job ahead of them in standardizing their breed. The earliest Bostons showed a wide diversity in type, especially where color, markings, size and head qualities were concerned as the Bulldog and the terrier combination was achieved.

In the earliest days, one of the principal problems was color. The Bull Terrier fanciers favored a white dog with brindle markings; the fanciers of the "new" Bull and terrier breed wanted a brindle and white dog, basically all brindle with white blaze and muzzle. Even before a written standard, the creators of the Boston Terrier had a definite picture in mind towards which they worked in their breeding operations. The rapid development of their breed's individuality and character over only a few decades was indeed notable and a credit to their purposeful procedures.

Creation of the head was probably the most difficult, considering the differences of the head of a Bulldog and of a terrier. A point of considerable early debate was the muzzle: should a slight tendency towards wrinkling be tolerated in order to achieve the short, blocky muzzle now so typical of the breed, or should a longer, weaker muzzle be excused to eliminate wrinkles? How can one achieve the desirable strength of muzzle in an even-jawed Boston? How can one achieve the correct Boston eye without a tendency towards a pop-eyed appearance? And what about the differences between the Bulldog and the terrier ear?

As the 1920's approached, a study was under way for the improvement of the then-existent standard, and the above were some of the questions under consideration. The original Boston Terrier standard had been drawn up in 1900, and revised with further elaboration on certain features in 1914. By 1919 many of the problems had been solved and the type firmly established towards the Boston Terrier we know today. Among these were the matter of size, which had been set originally at about 20 to 25 pounds. The first written standard had provided greater leeway, with three classes: under 15 pounds; under 25 pounds, and under 36 pounds. Later these classes were changed to 15-23 pounds; and 23-30

Ch. Grant's Fancy Command, by Ch. Grant's Royal Command ex Dale's Darling Duchess, bred by Dale E. Tromp and owned by Leonard L. Myers, Denver, Colorado. Photographed here in 1960, Fancy Command was winner of the Chicago and Philadelphia Specialties. This Best in Non-Sporting Group at Denver, is the dam of Ch. Command's Fancy Salute and Ch. Carry On Command.

pounds. Then came the period where commercial interests started to rear their ugly heads and a move got under way to create what amounted to Toy Boston Terriers, weighing in at between 9 and 12 pounds. Then in 1900 the bottom limit on the 15-23 pound class was lowered to 12 pounds. The latter tendency caused great concern to those interested purely in the protection of the breed quality as obviously the production on a large scale of what amounted to runts or dwarfs would be damaging breed type, stamina, and intelligence. Prompt action was taken in the form of another change in size classification: under 17 pounds, 17-22 pounds, and 22-27 pounds.

Basically there have been few changes in the Boston Terrier standards from the very beginning until the present time. Then, as now, General Appearance was described as a "lively, highly intelligent, smooth coated, compactly built, short tailed well balanced dog of medium station. The head should indicate a high degree of intelligence, in proportion to the size of the dog; body rather short and well knit; limbs strong and neatly turned; tail short; and no feature so prominent that the dog appears badly proportioned."

In the early 1900's it was noted that the matter of color, especially regarding markings, was not really explicit. The earliest dogs were light golden brindle with a considerable amount of white which soon gave way to mahogany brindle, with well placed markings the goal of the majority of breeders. Then came seal brindle, which color with proper markings made a dog especially desirable. As the shades of brindle became increasingly darker, so did a tendency towards the undesirable color of solid black on these correctly brindle parts of the dog.

Studying the early Boston Terrier photos, one can see quite easily the outstanding accomplishments of the breeders in creating quality and in perfecting their early dream of an ideal dog in which to take pride. The standards have kept pace with the needs of the breed, which have been more than anything a refinement and enhancement of the earliest dogs leading to the outstanding quality of later years.

As the original standard for Boston Terriers was drawn up in the United States, our breed standards throughout the world are principally based upon this one. Probably the chief difference has to do with ear cropping. In the countries where ear cropping is illegal, only a natural ear is acceptable. Elsewhere, both cropped or natural "bat" ears are permissible.

AMERICAN KENNEL CLUB STANDARD FOR THE BOSTON TERRIER

GENERAL APPEARANCE: The general appearance of the Boston Terrier should be that of a lively, highly intelligent, smooth-coated, short-headed, compactly built, short-tailed, well-balanced dog of medium station, of brindle color and evenly marked with white. The head should indicate a high degree of intelligence, and should be in proportion to the size of the dog; the body rather short and well knit, the limbs strong and neatly turned; tail short; and no feature be so prominent that the dog appears badly proportioned. The dog should convey an impression of determination, strength, and activity, with style of a high order; carriage easy and graceful. A proportionate combination of "color" and "ideal markings" is a particularly distinctive feature of a representative specimen, and a dog with a preponderance of white on body, or without the proper proportion of brindle and white on head, should possess sufficient merit otherwise to counteract its deficiencies in these respects. The ideal "Boston Terrier expression" as indicating "a high degree of intelligence," is also an important characteristic of the breed. "Color and markings" and "expression" should be given particular consideration in determining the relative value of "general appearance" to other points.

SKULL: Square, flat on top, free from wrinkles; cheeks flat; brows abrupt, stop well defined. *Eyes*—Wide apart, large and round, dark in color, expression alert, but kind and intelligent. The eyes should set square in the skull, and the outside corners should be on a line with the cheeks as viewed from the front. *Muzzle*—Short, square, wide and deep, and in proportion to skull; free from wrinkles; shorter in length than in width and depth, not exceeding in length approximately one third of length of skull; width and depth carried out well to end; the muzzle from stop to end of nose on a line parallel to the top of the skull; nose black and wide, with well defined line between nostrils. The jaws broad and square, with short regular teeth. Bite even or suffi-

Ch. Clasen's Cover Girl, by Clasen's Toy Blend ex Clasen's Doodles, was owned by Mr. and Mrs. Harry N. Clasen. In 1964, this pictured appeared in the then published *Popular Dogs* magazine in a feature titled "Rights and Wrongs in Boston Terriers" with the following caption: "The kind you like to judge. The near-perfect Boston. Beautiful head, topline, body and markings." These words are as true today as they were then.

Ch. Sunnyhaven's Mad Hatter, owned by Mrs. H. E. Edwards, winning Best of Breed at the Boston Terrier Club of Maryland Specialty in April 1961. Club President, Mrs. Elsie Koenigsberg, presenting the trophy.

ciently undershot to square muzzle. The chops of good depth but not pendulous, completely covering the teeth when mouth is closed. *Ears*—Carried erect, either cropped to conform to the shape of head, or natural bat, situated as near the corners of skull as possible.

HEAD FAULTS—Skull "domed" or inclined; furrowed by a medial line; skull too long for breadth, or vice versa; stop too shallow; brow and skull too slanting. Eyes small or sunken; too prominent; light color or walleye; showing too much white or haw. Muzzle wedge-shaped or lacking depth; down-faced; too much cut out below the eyes; pinched or wide nostrils; butterfly nose; protruding teeth; weak lower jaw; showing turn-up, layback, or wrinkled. Ears poorly carried or in size out of proportion to head.

NECK: Of fair length, slightly arched and carrying the head gracefully; setting neatly into shoulders. NECK FAULTS—Ewe necked; throatiness; short and thick.

BODY: Deep with good width of chest; shoulders sloping; back short; ribs deep and well sprung, carried well back to loins; loins short and muscular; rump curving slightly to set-on of tail; flank very slightly cut up. The body should appear short but not chunky. BODY FAULTS—Flat sides; narrow chest; long or slack loins; roach back; sway back; too much cut up in flank.

ELBOWS: Standing neither in nor out. *Forelegs*—Set moderately wide apart and on a line with the point of the shoulders; straight in bone and well muscled; pasterns short and strong. *Hind Legs*—Set true; bent at stifles; short from hocks to feet; hocks turning neither in nor out; thighs strong and well muscled. *Feet*—Round, small and compact and turned neither in nor out; toes well arched.

LEG AND FEET FAULTS—Loose shoulders or elbows; hind legs too straight at stifles; hocks too prominent; long or weak pasterns; splay feet.

GAIT: The gait of the Boston Terrier is that of a sure-footed, straight-gaited dog, forelegs and hind legs moving straight ahead in line with perfect rhythm, each step indicating grace with power. GAIT FAULTS—There should be no rolling, paddling or weaving when gaited and any crossing movement, either front or rear, is a serious fault.

TAIL: Set-on low; short, fine and tapering; straight; or screw;

The exquisite Boston Terrier bitch, Ch. Clasen's Bit O'Honey, handled by Harry N. Clasen for Joe Glaser of New York City, here is winning Best of Breed at the Boston Terrier Club of New Jersey Specialty Show in November 1952. Bostons were great favorites with this famed theatrical agent, who always had some top ones being shown for him at the important events.

devoid of fringe or coarse hair, and not carried above horizontal. TAIL FAULTS—A long or gaily carried tail; extremely gnarled or curled against body. (Note—The preferred tail should not exceed in length approximately half the distance from set-on to hock).

IDEAL COLOR: Brindle with white markings. The brindle to be evenly distributed and distinct. Black with white markings permissible but brindle with white markings preferred. *Ideal markings*—White muzzle, even white blaze over head, collar, breast, part or whole of forelegs, and hind legs below hocks. COLOR AND MARKINGS FAULTS—All white; absence of white marking; preponderance of white on body; without the proper proportion of brindle and white on head; or any variations detracting from the general appearance.

COAT: Short, smooth, bright and fine in texture. COAT FAULTS—Long or coarse; lacking luster.

WEIGHT: Not exceeding 25 pounds, divided by classes as follows; lightweight, under 15 pounds; middleweight, 15 and under 20 pounds; heavyweight, 20 and not exceeding 25 pounds.

Scale of Points

GENERAL APPEARANCE	10
SKULL	10
EYES	5
MUZZLE	10
EARS	2
NECK	3
BODY	15
ELBOWS	4
FORELEGS	5
HIND LEGS	5
GAIT	10
FEET	5
TAIL	5
COLOR	4
IDEAL MARKINGS	5
COAT	2
TOTAL	100

Disqualifications: Solid black; black and tan; liver or mouse colors. Dudley nose. Docked tail or any artificial means used to deceive the judge. Approved, April 9, 1957.

KENNEL CLUB (GREAT BRITAIN) VARIATION TO STANDARD

The British Standard for the Boston Terrier is written basically along the same lines as that of the American Kennel Club with the following differences:

1) Ear cropping is illegal in Great Britain, thus in that country only the natural ears are permitted under their standard, while in the United States they can be either cropped to conform to the shape of the head or they can be left natural. The majority of Boston Terriers shown in the United States do have cropped ears, although uncropped dogs, demanded in Great Britain, do appear occasionally at the American Kennel Club Shows as well.

2) No disqualifications are listed in the British Standard.

3) The British Standard does not include a Scale of Points.

Basically, however, the Standards are saying the same things about the dog, with the exception of ears.

The great and influential Ch. Zodiac's Special Beau, (December 1978-August 1984) who has contributed so tremendously to the modern Boston Terrier, was owned by Robert L. Breum, Omaha, Nebraska. By Ch. Unique's Special Beau ex Ch. Unique's Star of Zodiac, this dog was bred by Juanita Camp.

186

Chapter 7

Correct Type in the Boston Terrier

If you are selecting a Boston Terrier to show, or with whom to start a breeding program, or are yourself preparing to judge the breed, one of your most important tools towards success will be a complete understanding of the meaning of the word "type" and its application to this particular breed of dog.

In the language of purebred dog fanciers, "type" and "characteristics" are synonymous, both referring to the physical appearance of the dog in addition to personality traits, talents and disposition. To be even more specific, by "type" is meant the composite of features making that particular breed of dog distinctive; setting it apart from all other breeds; and making it easily recognizable as such.

To be strong in breed character, or of good type, a dog must adhere not only in personality but in conformation as well to what is considered ideal for his breed, this "ideal" being as described in the Boston Terrier Standard, which outlines the perfection which breeders are seeking to attain.

Boston Terrier fanciers are fortunate in that the Standard for this breed gives a "point rating" for each feature and thus helps outline for the novice exactly which features are to be considered the more important in evaluating the quality of one of these dogs. For example, any breed which allots a total of 27 points to the head is definitely what is known as a "head breed," a dog being more than one quarter on the way to perfection if that headpiece is as described in all detail. Obviously, under these circumstances it is difficult, if not impossible, for a poorly headed Boston Terrier to gain a championship, or any important recognition in the show ring.

With this in mind, let us consider what, exactly, creates an ideal Boston Terrier head. As the Standard tells us, the skull must be flat on top, free from wrinkles, flat over the cheek area, brow abrupt, and stop well defined — supporting all this, a broad, strong underjaw. The skull should really be thought of almost as resembling a cube in that the top and sides are perfectly flat with no roundness or bulge, the effect enhanced by correct placement of eyes and ears. The muzzle, or foreface, carry out this effect since the muzzle, which must be one third (1/3) or less the length of the skull, must carry out this same look of width and depth, with the area from stop to end of nose parallel to the top skull. No matter from which direction you look at it, the Boston head should not appear to "fall away." There is just as much strength proportionately in width and depth of foreface as of skull, and even the black nostrils are wide and large with a well defined line between them.

The bite may be even or of sufficient degree undershot, to square the muzzle.

General appearance usually translates "well balanced," as a show dog must look "all of a piece" with each part seeming appropriate to the rest of the dog. Thus the skull and foreface balance; the neck must be of correct length and strength to carry the head well and look in proportion to the size of the head and the length of the body. The body and legs should create an impression of balance by being of correct length and substance to make the dog short backed, never overly long bodied nor too highset or "leggy." The manner in which the dog travels is also part of "general appearance"; he should step smartly along, sure footed and agile. Ideal markings, too, come within this area, as surely nothing more beautifully enhances appearance than lovely, even, well placed snow-white markings.

How a great future Boston Terrier looks at the age of 12 weeks. This is the famous late Ch. Zodiac's Special Beau as a puppy. Courtesy of his breeder, Juanita Camp, Zodiac Bostons, Des Moines, Iowa.

Another distinct feature of the Boston Terrier is the tail. Correctly it should hang not more than half the distance between base and hock-joint; should be either straight or screw, free of fringe or coarse hair, and never carried higher than horizontal. An incorrectly carried tail can wreak havoc with general appearance as well as be a fault in itself.

Poor fronts are among the tenacious faults in this breed, although much progress has been made in overcoming them. Always remember that the forelegs of a Boston Terrier should be straight on a line with the shoulder, ending in strong, short pasterns and small, compact feet which turn neither in nor out, with elbows firm. Splay (spread) feet are an especially unattractive

Ch. Chahary Beau-K Lalka Karima, daughter of Ch. Beau Kay's Gay Chappie ex Ch. Chahary Beau Kay Kireielle, bred, owned, and handled by Ira Smoluchowski, Chahary Kennels, Rockford, Illinois. Won five Bests of Breed on the way to her title, and is the producer of many champions.

fault, as are fronts fringing on the "fiddle front" designation which end with the toes pointing outward as the pasterns approach one another. With 14 points designated for the elbows, forelegs and feet, these areas are *important*.

Hindquarters are strong and muscular, bent at the stifles and short from the hock joint to feet, hocks turning neither in nor out. The dog's strength of propelling power is dependent on proper assemblage of the hindlegs, proper "drive" resulting from correct angulation.

Shoulders should be well angulated (laid back), providing the length of reach to match the drive behind.

The ideal body is short but not chunky, (or cobby) in appearance. The chest is both deep and moderately broad, although never so broad as to interfere with free movement of the forelegs.

The short, muscular loins are important to correct body conformation, as is the slight cut-up at flank which lightens a chunky look, but should not be overdone. Rump curving *slightly* to set-on of tail is correct; but remember that a roached back (with which this should not be confused) and sway back are both faults themselves and detract from general appearance.

We hope that these comments will make it easier for you to picture the ideal Boston Terrier described so well in the Standard; and to recognize which areas are the more important in the evaluation of single members of the breed and in making comparisons among several.

Chapter 8

The Boston Terrier as a Family Dog

It was not without just cause and good reason that the Boston Terrier earned for himself, many years ago, the designation "American Gentleman" — for that he is in the canine world — exhibiting all the kindness, good manners and fastidious behavior one associates with a true gentleman.

There are many people who would like to have a large dog but for whom this is an impossibility. Such a person will find great pleasure in the ownership of a Boston Terrier, for here is one of the dogs who, although small in size, is large in doggy character, bringing to your home pleasant companionship, beauty, calm behavior, and a great deal of common sense. This is no little "yappy" lap dog. This is an intelligent, sensible, easily managed small dog who, although your lap may be among his favorite places, has many other sides to his personality as well.

Boston Terriers are fastidiously clean, tidy, and quiet to have around the house. They bear no "doggy" odor, and require no more than the barest minimum of grooming to keep their sparkling appearance. They are noted for their loving, affectionate personality, which includes devotion to family and friends, children, and your other pets. Boston Terriers seldom, if ever, are known to instigate fights (fortunate, as their large eyes are vulnerable and can easily be injured) but on the contrary are as loving and gentle towards other dogs as they are towards people. To quote some breeders I know who own them, "they have golden hearts and seem to smile a lot," "they are playful and forgiving with other dogs rather than vindictive," and, as for their intelligence, Boston owners always can be counted on to cite outstanding examples of the many ways in which Bostons of their acquaintance have proven themselves unusually keen in this regard.

The Boston Terrier is very much a family dog: sociable, loving, truly a "people dog" who will show affection for your friends and family as well as for you personally. They love and get on well with children (who should be taught to treat them gently and with respect, since they are small dogs who can be hurt by an overly rough or enthusiastic "game with the kids"), and they fraternize well with other Bostons, with dogs generally, and even with cats (who, with their claws, could, however be dangerous to their prominent and vulnerable eyes should too much play or a misunderstanding arise).

If it is at all possible, you would find the ownership of *two* Bostons as household pets twice as much fun as just one dog alone. They get on so well together that they are great company for one another, and their games and antics are amusing. Also this is a breed where two can be walked on leads together with no problem, which even makes exercising a couple just as easy as only one.

As are so many of the small breeds, Bostons are alert and "on the job" watchdogs, and can be counted on to announce any strange or suspicious activities around their home. They don't miss a trick, thus are quick to give the alarm should any prowler or other suspicious person or happening arise. True, being small they may not bring terror to the heart of an intruder, except that one of the most objectionable problems to a burglar or other person bent on mischief is noise to attract attention; and this the small dogs, including Bostons, are quick and loud to provide when something which seems to them suspicious comes along.

I honestly cannot think of any circumstances under which an average family dog is wanted that a Boston Terrier would not admirably "fill the bill." Obviously, they are not field or sporting

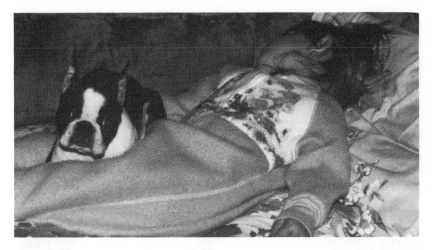

Ch. Blazermin's Family Tradition on guard over her best friend.

dogs; but as all-round household members they will bring count-less rewards and pleasures to you and your family by their person-ality, cleverness, and many endearing traits. Their handsome appearance cannot help but be a source of pride; their good man-ners add to the enjoyment of having them around; and their loyal-ity and understanding, demanding only your love, are among the finest rewards of dog ownership.

Bostons are sophisticated little fellows who like to travel (and are easy to take with you in their small carriers); enjoy going with you in the car; and meet with admiration and new friends when you take them along on walks for socialization. Whatever you would like to have them do, they will try their best and usually succeed. As we said previously, they are not field dogs, but short of that, nothing seems beyond them.

There is just one "caution area" in everyday living with a Bos-ton Terrier. This is the fact that those big, beautiful, full, round eyes which melt our hearts practically on sight are vulnerable to injury. A blow or scratch to an eye can cause painful problems; also eye irritations can result from exposure to tall grasses, pollen, twigs, or other such matters which can be encountered if the dog spends much time outdoors. So the eyes should be watched care-fully, and if injury or irritation occurs, the dog should be taken *promptly* to the veterinarian for proper treatment.

193

This is Ch. Jeffords' Constance, a young Boston Terrier of promise, who grew up to become a very famous winner, photographed as a puppy in 1976. Michael Wolf handling for himself and Mrs. Walter Jeffords.

194

Chapter 9

The Purchase of Your Boston Terrier

Careful consideration should be given to what breed of dog you wish to own prior to your purchase of one. If several breeds are attractive to you, and you are undecided as to which you prefer, learn all you can about the characteristics of each before making your decision. As you do so, you are thus preparing yourself to make an intelligent choice; and this is very important when buying a dog who will be, with reasonable luck, a member of your household for at least a dozen years or more. Obviously since you are reading this book, you have decided on the breed—so now all that remains is to make a good choice.

It is never wise to just rush out and buy the first cute puppy who catches your eye. Whether you wish a dog to show, one with whom to compete in obedience, or one as a family dog purely for his (or her) companionship, the more time and thought you invest as you plan the purchase, the more likely you are to meet with complete satisfaction. The background and early care behind your pet will reflect in the dog's future health and temperament. Even if you are planning the purchase purely as a pet, with no thoughts of showing or breeding in the dog's or puppy's future, it is essential that if the dog is to enjoy a trouble-free future you assure yourself of a healthy, properly raised puppy or adult from sturdy, well-bred stock.

Throughout the pages of this book you will find the names and locations of many well-known and well-established kennels in various areas. Another source of information is the American Kennel Club (51 Madison Avenue, New York, New York 10010) from whom you can obtain a list of recognized breeders in the vicinity of your home. If you plan to have your dog campaigned by a professional handler, by all means let the handler help you locate and select a good dog. Through their numerous clients, handlers have access to a variety of interesting show prospects; and the usual arrangement is that the handler re-sells the dog to you for what his cost has been, with the agreement that the dog be campaigned for you by him throughout the dog's career. It is most strongly recommended that prospective purchasers follow these suggestions, as you thus will be better able to locate and select a satisfactory puppy or dog.

Your first step in searching for your puppy is to make appointments at kennels specializing in your breed, where you can visit and inspect the dogs, both those available for sale and the kennel's basic breeding stock. You are looking for an active, sturdy puppy with bright eyes and intelligent expression and who is friendly and alert; avoid puppies who are hyperactive, dull, or listless. The coat should be clean and thick, with no sign of parasites. The premises on which he was raised should look (and smell) clean and be tidy, making it obvious that the puppies and their surroundings are in capable hands. Should the kennels featuring the breed you intend owning be sparse in your area or not have what you consider attractive, do not hesitate to contact others at a distance and purchase from them if they seem better able to supply a puppy or dog who will please you—*so long as it is a recognized breeding kennel of that breed.* Shipping dogs is a regular practice nowadays, with comparatively few problems when one considers the number of dogs shipped each year. A reputable, well-known breeder wants the customer to be satisfied; thus, he will represent the puppy fairly. Should you not be pleased with the puppy upon arrival, a

This is Kiss Me Kate Regardless at age five weeks appearing nationwide on postcards. A daughter of Ch. Gentleman Jim Regardless ex Lingrens Tutsey, she is the dam of littermates Ch. Showbiz Prima Donna and Ch. Showbiz Romeo. Owners, Lillian and Arthur Huddleston, Northridge, California.

Ch. Good Time Charlie T. Brown, No. I Boston Terrier; No. 10 Non-Sporting Dog for 1976, owned by Tom and Jackie Enwright, Winter Haven, Florida.

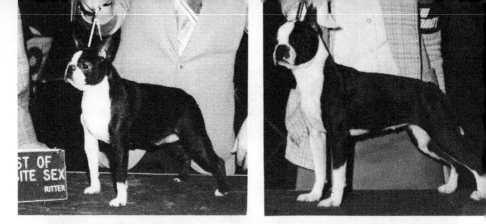

Left: Ch. Chahary Sonata Christinelli, bred and owned by Ira Smoluchowski, Rockford, Illinois. By Ch. Hogarth of Bar None ex Ch.Chahary Une Baiser Moi Kismet, finished her championship with four majors, including the Fort Wayne Boston Terrier Club Specialty (five points). *Right:* Ch. Clasen's Joy, by Ch. Toby Junior II ex Clasen's Fantastic Lady, the dam of Ch. Scott's Stuff-N-Nonsense, finished with a five-point major taking Best of Opposite Sex over specials. Bred and owned by Barbara Scott, Scott's Boston Terriers, Lillington, North Carolina.

Ch. Unique's Star of Zodiac, by Ch. Unique's Royalty Kid ex Vogel's Velvet Cover Girl, is the dam of Ch. Zodiac's Special Beau. Bred and handled by Juanita Camp.

198

breeder, such as described, will almost certainly permit its return. A conscientious breeder takes real interest and concern in the welfare of the dogs he or she causes to be brought into the world. Such a breeder also is proud of a reputation for integrity. Thus on two counts, for the sake of the dog's future and the breeder's reputation, to such a person a *satisfied* customer takes precedence over a sale at any cost.

If your puppy is to be a pet or "family dog," the earlier the age at which it joins your household the better. Puppies are weaned and ready to start out on their own, under the care of a sensible new owner, at about six weeks old; and if you take a young one, it is often easier to train it to the routine of your household and to your requirements of it than is the case with an older dog which, even though still a puppy technically, may have already started habits you will find difficult to change. The younger puppy is usually less costly, too, as it stands to reason the breeder will not have as much expense invested in it. Obviously, a puppy that has been raised to five or six months old represents more in care and cash expenditure on the breeder's part than one sold earlier and therefore should be and generally is priced accordingly.

There is an enormous amount of truth in the statement that "bargain" puppies seldom turn out to be that. A "cheap" puppy, cheaply raised purely for sale and profit, can and often does lead to great heartbreak, including problems and veterinarian's bills which can add up to many times the initial cost of a properly reared dog. On the other hand, just because a puppy is expensive does not assure one that is healthy and well reared. There have been numerous cases where unscrupulous dealers have sold for several hundred dollars puppies that were sickly, in poor condition, and such poor specimens that the breed of which they were supposedly members was barely recognizable. So one cannot always judge a puppy by price alone. Common sense must guide a prospective purchaser, plus the selection of a *reliable*, well-recommended dealer whom you know to have well-satisfied customers or, best of all, a specialized breeder. You will probably find the fairest pricing at the kennel of a breeder. Such a person, experienced with the breed in general and with his or her own stock in particular, through extensive association with these dogs has watched enough of them mature to have obviously learned to assess quite accurately each puppy's potential—something impossible where such background is non-existent.

One more word on the subject of pets. Bitches make a fine choice for this purpose as they are usually quieter and more gentle than the males, easier to house train, more affectionate, and less inclined to roam. If you do select a bitch and have no intention of breeding or showing her, by all means have her spayed, for your sake and for hers. The advantages to the owner of a spayed bitch include avoiding the nuisance of "in season" periods which normally occur twice yearly, with the accompanying eager canine swains haunting your premises in an effort to get close to your female; plus the unavoidable messiness and spotting of furniture and rugs at this time, which can be annoying if she is a household companion in the habit of sharing your sofa or bed. As for the spayed bitch, she benefits as she grows older because this simple operation almost entirely eliminates the possibility of breast cancer ever occurring. It is recommended that all bitches eventually be spayed—even those used for show or breeding when their careers have ended—in order that they may enjoy a happier, healthier old age. Please take note, however, that a bitch who has been spayed (or an altered dog) *cannot be shown at American Kennel Club dog shows once this operation has been performed.* Be certain that you are *not* interested in showing her before taking this step.

Also, in selecting a pet, never underestimate the advantages of an older dog, perhaps a retired show dog or a bitch no longer needed for breeding, who may be available quite reasonably priced by a breeder anxious to place such a dog in a loving home. These dogs are settled and can be a delight to own, as they make wonderful companions, especially in a household of adults where raising a puppy can sometimes be a trial.

Everything that has been said about careful selection of your pet puppy and its place of purchase applies, but with many further considerations, when you plan to buy a show dog or foundation stock for a future breeding program. Now is the time for an in-depth study of the breed, starting with every word and every illustration in this book and all others you can find written on the subject. The Standard of the breed now has become your guide, and you must learn not only the words but also how to interpret them and how they are applicable in actual dogs before you are ready to make an intelligent selection of a show dog.

If you are thinking in terms of a dog to show, obviously you must have learned about dog shows and must be in the habit of attending them. This is fine, but now your activity in this direction should be increased, with your attending every single dog show within a reasonable distance from your home. Much can be learned about a breed at ringside at these events. Talk with the breeders who are exhibiting. Study the dogs they are showing. Watch the judging with concentration, noting each decision made, and attempt to follow the reasoning by which the judge has reached it. Note carefully the attributes of the dogs who win and, for your later use, the manner in which each is presented. Close your ears to the ringside know-it-alls, usually novice owners of only a dog or two and very new to the Fancy, who have only derogatory remarks to make about all that is taking place unless they happen to win. This is the type of exhibitor who "comes and goes" through the Fancy and whose interest is usually of very short duration owing to lack of knowledge and dissatisfaction caused by the failure to recognize the need to learn. You, as a fancier whom we hope will last and enjoy our sport over many future years, should develop independent thinking at this stage; you should learn to draw your own conclusions about the merits, or lack of them, seen before you in the ring and, thus, sharpen your own judgement in preparation for choosing wisely and well.

Note carefully which breeders campaign winning dogs, not just an occasional isolated good one, but consistent, homebred winners. It is from one of these people that you should select your own future "star."

If you are located in an area where dog shows take place only occasionally or where there are long travel distances involved, you will need to find another testing ground for your ability to select a worthy show dog. Possibly, there are some representative kennels raising this breed within a reasonable distance. If so, by all means ask permission of the owners to visit the kennels and do so when permission is granted. You may not necessarily buy then and there, as they may not have available what you are seeking that very day, but you will be able to see the type of dog being raised there and to discuss the dogs with the breeder. Every time you do this, you add to your knowledge. Should one of these kennels have dogs which especially appeal to you, perhaps you could reserve a show-prospect puppy from a coming litter. This is frequently done, and it is often worth waiting for a puppy, unless you have seen a dog with which you truly are greatly impressed and which is immediately available.

The purchase of a puppy has already been discussed. Obviously this same approach applies in a far greater degree when the purchase involved is a future show dog. The only place at which to purchase a show prospect is from a breeder who raises show-type stock; otherwise, you are almost certainly doomed to disappointment as the puppy matures. Show and breeding kennels obviously cannot keep all of their fine young stock. An active breeder-exhibitor is, therefore, happy to place promising youngsters in the hands of people also interested in showing and winning with them, doing so at a fair price according to the quality and prospects of the dog involved. Here again, if no kennel in your immediate area has what you are seeking, do not hesitate to contact top breeders in other areas and to buy at long distance. Ask for pictures, pedigrees, and a complete description. Heed the breeder's advice and recommendations, after truthfully telling exactly what your expectations are for the dog you purchase. Do you want something with which to win just a few ribbons now and then? Do you want a dog who can complete his championship? Are you thinking of the real "big time" (*i.e.*, seriously campaigning with Best of Breed, Group wins, and possibly even Best in Show as your eventual goal)? Consider it all carefully in advance; then honestly discuss your plans with the breeder. You will be better satisfied with the results if you do this, as the breeder is then in the best position to help you choose the dog who is most likely to come through for you. A breeder selling a show dog is just as anxious as the buyer for the dog to succeed, and the breeder will represent the dog to you with truth and honesty. Also, this type of breeder does not lose interest the moment the sale has been made but when necessary will be right there ready to assist you with beneficial advice and suggestions based on years of experience.

As you make inquiries of at least several kennels, keep in mind that show-prospect puppies are less expensive than mature show dogs, the latter often costing close to four figures, and sometimes

Ch. Griffing's Little Chappie, a noted star of the late 1940's, by Ch. Hayes Diplomat ex Griffing's Miracle Madcap, bred by Anne and Bob Griffing, later sold to Signe A. Carlson. Chappie sired a total of 19 champions, five of whom were all-breed Best in Show winners: Ch. Chappie's Little Man, Ch. Silver's Fancy Chap, Ch. The Black Eyed Imp, Ch. Chappie' Regards, and Ch. Chappie's Defender. These, and several other of his champions, made impressive wins at Specialty Shows and in Group competition. Chappie won five Groups after purchase by Miss Carlson, and a Best in Show under Mrs. Beatrice Godsol. Photo courtesy of Leonard L. Myers.

Ch. Montecalvo's Little Whiz II, owned by Frank Montecalvo and handled by Albert Rosenbloom, here is winning the Specialty Show of the Boston Terrier Club of New York in 1963 judged by Leonard L. Myers. This handsome little dog was later sold to England, where we feel certain he proved a valuable asset to those interested in breeding quality Boston Terriers.

more. The reason for this is that, with a puppy, there is always an element of chance, the possibility of it's developing unexpected faults as it matures or failing to develop the excellence and quality that earlier had seemed probable. There definitely is a risk factor in buying a show-prospect puppy. Sometimes all goes well, but occasionally the swan becomes an ugly duckling. Reflect on this as you consider available puppies and young adults. It just might be a good idea to go with a more mature, though more costly, dog if one you like is available.

When you buy a mature show dog, "what you see is what you get," and it is not likely to change beyond coat and condition which are dependent on your care. Also advantageous for a novice owner is the fact that a mature dog of show quality almost certainly will have received show-ring training and probably match-show experience, which will make your earliest handling ventures far easier.

Frequently it is possible to purchase a beautiful dog who has completed championship but who, owing to similarity in bloodlines, is not needed for the breeder's future program. Here you have the opportunity of owning a champion, usually in the two-to-five-year-old range, which you can enjoy campaigning as a special (for Best of Breed competition) and which will be a settled, handsome dog for you and your family to enjoy with pride.

If you are planning foundation for a future kennel, concentrate on acquiring one or two really superior bitches. These need not necessarily be top show-quality, but they should represent your breed's finest producing bloodlines from a strain noted for producing quality, generation after generation. A proven matron who is already the dam of show-type puppies is, of course, the ideal selection; but these are usually difficult to obtain, no one being anxious to part with so valuable an asset. You just might strike it lucky, though, in which case you are off to a flying start. If you cannot find such a matron available, select a young bitch of finest background from top-producing lines who is herself of decent type, free of obvious faults, and of good quality.

Great attention should be paid to the pedigree of the bitch from whom you intend to breed. If not already known to you, try to see the sire and dam. It is generally agreed that someone starting with a breed should concentrate on a fine collection of topflight bitches and raise a few litters from these before considering keeping one's own stud dog. The practice of buying a stud and then breeding everything you own or acquire to that dog does not always work out well. It is better to take advantage of the many noted sires who are available to be used at stud, who represent all of the leading strains, and in each case to carefully select the one who in type and pedigree seems most compatible to each of your bitches, at least for your first several litters.

To summarize, if you want a "family dog" as a companion, it is best to buy it young and raise it according to the habits of your household. If you are buying a show dog, the more mature it is, the more certain you can be of its future beauty. If you are buying foundation stock for a kennel, then bitches are better, but they must be from the finest *producing* bloodlines.

When you buy a pure-bred dog that you are told is eligible for registration with the American Kennel Club, you are entitled to receive from the seller an application form which will enable you to register your dog. If the seller cannot give you the application form you should demand and receive an identification of your dog consisting of the name of the breed, the registered names and numbers of the sire and dam, the name of the breeder, and your dog's date of birth. If the litter of which your dog is a part is already recorded with the American Kennel Club, then the litter number is sufficient identification.

Do not be misled by promises of papers at some later date. Demand a registration application form or proper identification as described above. If neither is supplied, do not buy the dog. So warns the American Kennel Club, and this is especially important in the purchase of show or breeding stock.

Talone's Bostons in their yard. Owned by John and Nancy Talone, Knoxville, Tennessee.

Game time. Four of the lovely homebreds at Barbara Scott's are enjoying a tug-of-war.

Chapter 10

The Care of Your Boston Terrier Puppy

The moment you decide to be the new owner of a puppy is not one second too soon to start planning for the puppy's arrival in your home. Both the new family member and you will find the transition period easier if your home is geared in advance of the arrival.

The first things to be prepared are a bed for the puppy and a place where you can pen him up for rest periods. Every dog should have a crate of its own from the very beginning, so that he will come to know and love it as his special place where he is safe and happy. It is an ideal arrangement, for when you want him to be free, the crate stays open. At other times you can securely latch it and know that the pup is safely out of mischief. If you travel with him, his crate comes along in the car; and, of course, in traveling by plane there is no alternative but to have a carrier for the dog. If you show your dog, you will want him upon occasion to be in a crate a good deal of the day. So from every consideration, a crate is a very sensible and sound investment in your puppy's future safety and happiness and for your own peace of mind.

The crates most desirable are the wooden ones with removable side panels, which are ideal for cold weather (with the panels in place to keep out drafts) and in hot weather (with the panels removed to allow better air circulation). Wire crates are all right in the summer, but they give no protection from cold or drafts. Aluminum crates, due to the manner in which the metal reflects surrounding temperatures, are not recommended. If it is cold, so is the metal of the crate; if it is hot, the crate becomes burning hot.

When you choose the puppy's crate, be certain that it is roomy enough not to become outgrown. The crate should have sufficient height so the dog can stand up in it as a mature dog and sufficient area so that he can stretch out full length when relaxed. When the puppy is young, first give him shredded newspaper as a bed; the papers can be replaced with a mat or turkish towels when the dog is older. Carpet remnants are great for the bottom of the crate, as they are inexpensive and in case of accidents can be quite easily replaced. As the dog matures and is past the chewing age, a pillow or blanket in the crate is an appreciated comfort.

Sharing importance with the crate is a safe area in which the puppy can exercise and play. If you are an apartment dweller, a baby's playpen works out well for a young dog; for an older puppy use a portable exercise pen which you can then use later when travelling with your dog or for dog shows. If you have a yard, an area where he can be outside in safety should be fenced in prior to the dog's arrival at your home. This area does not need to be huge, but it does need to be made safe and secure. If you are in a suburban area where there are close neighbors, stockade fencing works out best as then the neighbors are less aware of the dog and the dog cannot see and bark at everything passing by. If you are out in the country where no problems with neighbors are likely to occur, then regular chain-link fencing is fine. For added precaution in both cases, use a row of concrete blocks or railroad ties inside against the entire bottom of the fence; this precludes or at least considerably lessens the chances of your dog digging his way out.

Be advised that if yours is a single dog, it is very unlikely that it will get sufficient exercise just sitting in the fenced area, which is what most of them do when they are there alone. Two or more dogs will play and move themselves around, but one by itself does

Accustom your puppies to the lead at an early age. Future Ch. Jeffords Sherlock Holmes here is already getting the hang of it at four months old. Owned by Honore Rosen, Park Ridge, New Jersey.

Boston puppies can be adventuresome, and learn at an early age to climb over the protective sides of their whelping box. Honore Rosen, owner, Park Ridge, New Jersey.

little more than make a leisurely tour once around the area to check things over and then lie down. You must include a daily walk or two in your plans if your puppy is to be rugged and well. Exercise is extremely important to a puppy's muscular development and to keep a mature dog fit and trim. So make sure that those exercise periods, or walks, a game of ball, and other such activities, are part of your daily program as a dog owner.

If your fenced area has an outside gate, provide a padlock and key and a strong fastening for it, and use them, so that the gate cannot be opened by others and the dog taken or turned free. The ultimate convenience in this regard is, of course, a door (unused for other purposes) from the house around which the fenced area can be enclosed, so that all you have to do is open the door and out into his area he goes. This arrangement is safest of all, as then you need not be using a gate, and it is easier in bad weather since then you can send the dog out without taking him and becoming soaked yourself at the same time. This is not always possible to manage, but if your house is arranged so that you could do it this way, you would never regret it due to the convenience and added safety thus provided. Fencing in the entire yard, with gates to be opened and closed whenever a caller, deliveryman, postman, or some other person comes on your property, really is not safe at all because people not used to gates and their importance are frequently careless about closing and latching them *securely*. Many heartbreaking incidents have been brought about by someone carelessly half closing a gate (which the owner had thought to be firmly latched) and the dog wandering out. For greatest security a fenced *area* definitely takes precedence over a fenced *yard*.

The puppy will need a collar (one that fits now, not one to be grown into) and a lead from the moment you bring him home. Both should be an appropriate weight and type for his size. Also needed are a feeding dish and a water dish, both made preferably of unbreakable material. Your pet supply shop should have an interesting assortment of these and other accessories from which you can choose. Then you will need grooming tools of the type the breeder recommends and some toys. Equally satisfactory is Nylabone®, a nylon bone that does not chip or splinter and that "frizzles" as the puppy chews, providing healthful gum massage.

Nylabones® are safe for all dogs to chew. Nylabones will not swell when wet, break up into pieces or get splintered, or cause allergic reactions. Choose the size that fits your dog's age and breed. Two kinds of flavors, meat and chocolate, are available. Nylabones are therapeutic products, not toys.

An appealing Boston puppy, toy in mouth, seems to be saying "come play with me." Owned by Terry Goss, Fenwick, Ontario, Canada.

Avoid plastics and any sort of rubber toys, *particularly those with squeakers* which the puppy may remove and swallow. If you want a ball for the puppy to use when playing with him, select one of very hard construction made for this purpose and do not leave it alone with him because he may chew off and swallow bits of the rubber. Take the ball with you when the game is over. This also applies to some of those "tug of war" type rubber toys which are fun when used with the two of you for that purpose but again should *not* be left behind for the dog to work on with his teeth. Bits of swallowed rubber, squeakers, and other such foreign articles can wreak great havoc in the intestinal tract—do all you can to guard against them.

Too many changes all at once can be difficult for a puppy. For at least the first few days he is with you, keep him on the food and feeding schedule to which he is accustomed. Find out ahead of time from the breeder what he feeds his puppies, how frequently, and at what times of the day. Also find out what, if any, food supplements the breeder has been using and recommends. Then be prepared by getting in a supply of the same food so that you will have it there when you bring the puppy home. Once the puppy is accustomed to his new surroundings, then you can switch the type of food and schedule to fit your convenience, but for the first several days do it as the puppy expects.

Your selection of a veterinarian also should be attended to before the puppy comes home, because you should stop at the vet's office for the puppy to be checked over as soon as you leave the breeder's premises. If the breeder is from your area, ask him for recommendations. Ask you dog-owning friends for their opinions of the local veterinarians, and see what their experiences with those available have been. Choose someone whom several of your friends recommend highly, then contact him about your puppy, perhaps making an appointment to stop in at his office. If the premises are clean, modern, and well equipped, and if you like the veterinarian, make an appointment to bring the puppy in on the day of purchase. Be sure to obtain the puppy's health record from the breeder, including information on such things as shots and worming that the puppy has had.

JOINING THE FAMILY

Remember that, exciting and happy an occasion as it is for you, the puppy's move from his place of birth to your home can be, for him, a traumatic experience. His mother and littermates will be missed. He quite likely will be awed or frightened by the change of surroundings. The person on whom he depended will be gone. Everything should be planned to make his arrival at your home pleasant—to give him confidence and to help him realize that yours is a pretty nice place to be after all.

Never bring a puppy home on a holiday. There just is too much going on with people and gifts and excitement. If he is in honor of an "occasion," work it out so that his arrival will be a few days earlier, or perhaps even better, a few days later than the "occasion." Then your home will be back to its normal routine and the puppy can enjoy your undivided attention. Try not to bring the puppy home in the evening. Early morning is the ideal time, as then he has the opportunity of getting acquainted and the initial strangeness should wear off before bedtime. You will find it a more peaceful night that way. Allow the puppy to investigate as he likes, under your watchful eye. If you already have a pet in the household, keep a careful watch that the relationship between the two gets off to a friendly start or you may quickly find yourself with a lasting problem. Much of the future attitude of each toward the other will depend on what takes place that first day, so keep your mind on what they are doing and let your other activities slide for the moment. Be careful not to let your older pet become jealous by paying more attention to the puppy than to him, as that will start a bad situation immediately.

If you have a child, here again it is important that the relationship start out well. Before the puppy is brought home, you should have a talk with the youngster. He must clearly understand that puppies are fragile and can easily be injured; therefore, they should not be teased, hurt, mauled, or overly rough-housed. A puppy is not an inanimate toy; it is a living thing with a right to be loved and handled respectfully, treatment which will reflect in the dog's attitude toward your child as both mature together. Never permit your children's playmates to mishandle the puppy, tormenting the puppy until it turns on the children in self-defense. Children often do not realize how rough is too rough. You, as a responsible adult, are obligated to assure that your puppy's relationship with children is a pleasant one.

Do not start out by spoiling your puppy. A puppy is usually pretty smart and can be quite demanding. What you had considered to be "just for tonight" may be accepted by the puppy as "for keeps." Be firm with him, strike a routine, and stick to it. The puppy will learn more quickly this way, and everyone will be happier as a result. A radio playing softly or a dim night light are often comforting to a puppy as it gets accustomed to new surroundings and should be provided in preference to bringing the puppy to bed with you—unless, of course, you intend him to share the bed as a permanent arrangement.

SOCIALIZING AND TRAINING

Socialization and training of your puppy should start the very day of his arrival in your home. Never address him without calling him by name. A short, simple name is the easiest to teach as it catches the dog's attention quickly, so avoid elaborate call names. Always address the dog by the same name, not a whole series of pet names; the latter will only confuse the puppy.

Use his name clearly, and call the puppy over to you when you see him awake and wandering about. When he comes, make a big fuss over him for being such a good dog. He thus will quickly associate the sound of his name with coming to you and a pleasant happening.

Several hours after the puppy's arrival is not too soon to start accustoming him to the feel of a light collar. He may hardly notice it; or he may struggle, roll over, and try to rub it off his neck with his paws. Divert his attention when this occurs by offering a tasty snack or a toy (starting a game with him) or by petting him. Before long he will have accepted the strange feeling around his neck and no longer appear aware of it. Next comes the lead. Attach it and then immediately take the puppy outside or otherwise try to divert his attention with things to see and sniff. He may struggle against the lead at first, biting at it and trying to free himself. Do not pull him with it at this point; just hold the end loosely and try to follow him if he starts off in any direction. Normally his attention will soon turn to investigating his sourroundings if he is outside or you have taken him into an unfamiliar room in your house; curiosity will take over and he will become interested in sniffing

A lovely photo of the beautiful bitch Ch. Country Kin Carmelina and her owner Honore Rosen informally taken at the shore. Marc and Honore Rosen, owners, Scotland Yard Kennels, Park Ridge, New Jersey.

Puppies by Ch. Talone's Ruff-N-Tuff ex Talone's Special Beau Brandy, born in 1985. Owned by John and Nancy Talone, Knoxville, Tennessee.

around the surroundings. Just follow him with the lead slackly held until he seems to have completely forgotten about it; then try with gentle urging to get him to follow you. Don't be rough or jerk at him; just tug gently on the lead in short quick motions (steady pulling can become a battle of wills), repeating his name or trying to get him to follow your hand which is holding a bite of food or an interesting toy. If you have an older lead-trained dog, then it should be a cinch to get the puppy to follow along after *him*. In any event the average puppy learns quite quickly and will soon be trotting along nicely on the lead. Once that point has been reached, the next step is to teach him to follow on your left side, or heel. Of course this will not likely be accomplished all in one day but should be done with short training periods over the course of several days until you are satisfied with the result.

During the course of house training your puppy, you will need to take him out frequently and at regular intervals: first thing in the morning directly from the crate, immediately after meals, after the puppy has been napping, or when you notice that the puppy is looking for a spot. Choose more or less the same place to take the puppy each time so that a pattern will be established. If he does not go immediately, do not return him to the house as he will probably relieve himself the moment he is inside. Stay out with him until he has finished; then be lavish with your praise for his good behavior. If you catch the puppy having an accident indoors, grab him firmly and rush him outside, sharply saying "No!" as you pick him up. If you do not see the accident occur, there is little point in doing anything except cleaning it up, as once it has happened and been forgotten, the puppy will most likely not even realize why you are scolding him.

Especially if you live in a big city or are away many hours at a time, having a dog that is trained to go on paper has some very definite advantages. To do this, one proceeds pretty much the same way as taking the puppy outdoors, except now you place the puppy on the newspaper at the proper time. The paper should always be kept in the same spot. An easy way to paper train a puppy if you have a playpen for it or an exercise pen is to line the area with newspapers; then gradually, every day or so, remove a section of newspaper until you are down to just one or two. The puppy acquires the habit of using the paper; and as the prepared

Puppies born in May 1977 by Ch. Victor of Bar None ex Champion Bicenten-
nial Belle of Bar None. Owned by Bar None Bostons, Robert L. Breum,
Omaha, Nebraska.

Blazermin's April in her training program, learning to "stack" nicely on the table. Sired By Ch. Staley's El-Bo's Showman ex Ch. Blazermin's Family Tradition, she is owned by the Cronens, Louisville, Kentucky.

area grows smaller, in the majority of cases the dog will continue to use whatever paper is still available. It is pleasant, if the dog is alone for an excessive length of time, to be able to feel that if he needs it the paper is there and will be used.

The puppy should form the habit of spending a certain amount of time in his crate, even when you are home. Sometimes the puppy will do this voluntarily, but if not, he should be taught to do so, which is accomplished by leading the puppy over by his collar, gently pushing him inside, and saying firmly, "Down" or "Stay." Whatever expression you use to give a command, stick to the very same one each time for each act. Repetition is the big thing in training—and so is association with what the dog is expected to do. When you mean "Sit," always say exactly that. "Stay" should mean *only* that the dog should remain where he receives the command. "Down" means something else again. Do not confuse the dog by shuffling the commands, as this will create training problems for you.

As soon as he had had his immunization shots, take your puppy with you whenever and wherever possible. There is nothing that will build a self-confident, stable dog like socialization, and it is extremely important that you plan and give the time and energy necessary for this whether your dog is to be a show dog or a pleasant, well-adjusted family member. Take your puppy in the car so that he will learn to enjoy riding and not become carsick, as dogs may do if they are infrequent travelers. Take him anywhere you are going where you are certain he will be welcome: visiting friends and relatives (if they do not have housepets who may resent the visit), busy shopping centers (keeping him always on lead), or just walking around the streets of your town. If someone admires him (as always seems to happen when one is out with puppies), encourage the stranger to pet and talk with him. Socialization of this type brings out the best in your puppy and helps him to grow up with a friendly outlook, liking the world and its inhabitants. The worst thing that can be done to a puppy's personality is to overly shelter him. By always keeping him at home away from things and people unfamiliar to him, you may be creating a personality problem for the mature dog that will be a cross for you to bear later on.

Ch. Fascinating Fancy Beau owned by Mary Alice Niebauer, Cassapolis, Michigan. This lovely dog, 1965-1978, enjoyed an exciting career in the United States after which he was sold to Helen Fottrell of Ireland where he became one of the United Kingdom's outstanding Boston Terrier sires.

FEEDING YOUR DOG

Time was when providing nourishing food for dogs involved a far more complicated procedure than people now feel is necessary. The old school of thought was that the daily ration must consist of fresh beef, vegetables, cereal, egg yolks, and cottage cheese as basics with such additions as brewer's yeast and vitamin tablets on a daily basis.

During recent years, however, many minds have changed regarding this procedure. Eggs, cottage cheese, and supplements to the diet are still given, but the basic method of feeding dogs has changed; and the change has been, in the opinion of many authorities, definitely for the better. The school of thought now is that you are doing your dogs a favor when you feed them some of the fine commerically prepared dog foods in preference to your own home-cooked concoctions.

The reason behind this new outlook is easily understandable. The dog food industry has grown to be a major one, participated in by some of the best known and most respected names in America. These trusted firms, it is agreed, turn out excellent products, so people are feeding their dog food preparations with confidence and the dogs are thriving, living longer, happier, and healthier lives than ever before. What more could one want?

There are at least half a dozen absolutely top-grade dry foods to be mixed with broth or water and served to your dog according to directions. There are all sorts of canned meats, and there are several kinds of "convenience foods," those in a packet which you open and dump out into the dog's dish. It is just that simple. The convenience foods are neat and easy to use when you are away from home, but generally speaking a dry food mixed with hot water (or soup) and meat is preferred. It is the opinion of many that the canned meat, with its added fortifiers, is more beneficial to the dogs than the fresh meat. However, the two can be alternated or, if you prefer and your dog does well on it, by all means use fresh ground beef. A dog enjoys changes in the meat part of his diet, which is easy with the canned food since all sorts of beef are available (chunk, ground, stewed, and so on), plus lamb, chicken, and even such concoctions as liver and egg, just plain liver flavor, and a blend of five meats.

There is also prepared food geared to every age bracket of your dog's life, from puppyhood on through old age, with special additions or modifications to make it particularly nourishing and beneficial. Previous generations never had it so good where the canine dinner is concerned, because these commercially prepared foods are tasty and geared to meeting the dog's gastronomic approval.

Additionally, contents and nutrients are clearly listed on the labels, as are careful instructions for feeding just the right amount for the size, weight, and age of each dog.

With these foods the addition of extra vitamins is not necessary, but if you prefer there are several kinds of those, too, that serve as taste treats as well as being beneficial. Your pet supplier has a full array of them.

Of course there is no reason not to cook up something for your dog if you would feel happier doing so. But it seems unnecessary when such truly satisfactory rations are available with so much less trouble and expense.

How often you feed your dog is a matter of how it works out best for you. Many owners prefer to do it once a day. It is generally agreed that two meals, each of smaller quantity, are better for the digestion and more satisfying to the dog, particularly if yours is a household member who stands around and watches preparations for the family meals. Do not overfeed. This is the shortest route to all sorts of problems. Follow directions and note carefully how your dog is looking. If your dog is overweight, cut back the quantity of food a bit. If the dog looks thin, then increase the amount. Each dog is an individual and the food intake should be adjusted to his requirements to keep him feeling and looking trim and in top condition.

From the time puppies are fully weaned until they are about twelve weeks old, they should be fed four times daily. From three months to six months of age, three meals should suffice. At six months of age the puppies can be fed two meals, and the twice daily feedings can be continued until the puppies are close to one year old, at which time feeding can be changed to once daily if desired. If you do feed just once a day, do so by early afternoon at the latest and give the dog a snack, a biscuit or two, at bedtime.

Remember that plenty of fresh water should always be available to your puppy or dog for drinking. This is of utmost importance to his health.

GROOMING YOUR BOSTON TERRIER

The Boston Terrier is one of the easiest dogs to manage where coat care and grooming are concerned. His smooth, short coat seldom requires tub bathing; and you will find quite satisfactory the results of using one of the commerical "dry" shampoos which are available from your pet supplier. These are used by spreading the product all over the dog, rubbing it into the coat, and then wiping dry with a turkish towel. You will most times find this sufficient to leave the dog sparkling clean, shining, and sweet smelling; and it can be done whenever necessary.

If you are preparing the dog for the show ring, you will need to take steps to whiten his markings, with final touches the last moment on the day of the show. To do this, French White Chalk is used on the white areas, especially the face. Bar or cake chalk is rubbed into the white area, and then a soft, natural bristle brush is used to remove it *entirely*. The use of white chalk is very common in breeds which have white in their coat pattern, as nothing else will obliterate the "grimy" look of leaving them "as is." But be forewarned: *every last bit* of this chalk *must be removed prior to entering the show ring,* as show rules are that the judge must disqualify any dog in whose coat traces of powder or chalk are found. So do not be careless in making sure that no traces of the chalk remain when you take your dog to the ring. It's not all that difficult, but requires your sharp attention while cleaning up traces of the whitening process. The last thing you ever want is for a judge to find himself with white smudges on his hands or jacket after examining *your* Boston Terrier.

Should you feel it necessary to bathe your Boston occasionally between the dry shampoos, use a shampoo recommended to you by your pet store owner or whatever product the breeder of your puppy recommends. Several of the brand-name products do an excellent job. Be sure to rinse thoroughly so as to avoid skin irritation by traces of soap left behind.

It is especially important in Bostons, owing to the size and prominence of their eyes, that a drop of castor oil be placed in each eye for protection from the soap before lathering up. Never forget to do this. Also place a wad of cotton in each ear to protect against water entering the ear canal.

Use mildly warm water (remember, your Boston is more vulnerable to "too hot" or "too cold" due to his short coat than are heavily coated breeds), and a good spray. You can either towel dry your Boston or use a hair dryer; if the latter, make certain that the temperature remains comfortable, and in either case blot out the excess moisture with a towel to begin the drying process.

An important part of grooming is proper care of the toenails. These should be clipped whenever necessary (and checked weekly), and never permitted to grow excessively long. Purchase a good quality nail clipper of size suitable for a Boston Terrier, and in using it be careful not to cut into the pink section of the nail (the "quick"), as doing so will cause bleeding. Should this happen, a touch of styptic powder on the end of the cut nail should stop the bleeding quickly.

Many professionals prefer to use an electric nail grinder with which to keep nails short and smooth. This method does leave a smoother finish, but some dogs may be frightened of the noise; and also caution should be used as it is easy to get the nails too short almost before you are aware of having done so.

A check of the ears at least once weekly should be included in grooming. Clean the ear gently with cotton-tipped swabs which have been dampened in peroxide or alcohol, being careful not to probe too deeply. Should the ear prove to be really dirty, have it checked by your veterinarian; also should there be any strong odor emanating from it. This is infrequent and unlikely, however, as Bostons are not prone to ear problems.

If you plan to show your Boston, he will look smarter and neater if his whiskers are kept trimmed close to the skin. For this you should have a good quality *curved* scissors, which will cut down the possibility of an accident to the eye during the process. Cut the whiskers as short, or close to the skin, as you can. They sometimes grow amazingly fast, so should be checked on the day of the show to be certain they have remained close cropped.

Talone's Tisket-N-Tasket, by Ch. Byron's T-N-T ex Ch. Talone's Topper-N-Tina, a homebred owned by John and Nancy Talone, Knoxville, Tennessee, taking Best of Winners for a four point major at Asheville 1979.

Chapter 11

The Making of a Show Dog

If you have decided to become a show dog exhibitor, you have accepted a very real and very exciting challenge. The groundwork has been accomplished with the selection of your future show prospect. If you have purchased a puppy, it is assumed that you have gone through all the proper preliminaries concerning good care, which should be the same if the puppy is a pet or future show dog, with a few added precautions for the latter.

GENERAL CONSIDERATIONS

Remember the importance of keeping your future winner in trim, top condition. Since you want him neither too fat nor too thin, his appetite for his proper diet should be guarded, and children and guests should not be permitted to constantly feed him "goodies." The best treat of all is a small wad of raw ground beef or a packaged dog treat. To be avoided are ice cream, cake, cookies, potato chips, and other fattening items which will cause the dog to put on weight and may additionally spoil his appetite for the proper, nourishing, well-balanced diet so essential to good health and condition.

The importance of temperament and showmanship cannot possibly be overestimated. They have put many a mediocre dog across, while lack of them can ruin the career of an otherwise outstanding specimen. From the day your dog joins your family, socialize him. Keep him accustomed to being with people and to being handled by people. Encourage your friends and relatives to "go over" him as the judges will in the ring so this will not seem a strange and upsetting experience. Practice showing his "bite" (the manner in which his teeth meet) quickly and deftly. It is quite simple to slip the lips apart with your fingers, and the puppy should be willing to accept this from you or the judge without struggle.

Some judges prefer that the exhibitors display the dog's bite and other mouth features themselves. These are the considerate ones, who do not wish to chance the spreading of possible infection from dog to dog with their hands on each one's mouth—a courtesy particularly appreciated in these days of virus epidemics. But the old-fashioned judges still persist in doing it themselves, so the dog should be ready for either possibility.

Take your future show dog with you in the car, thus accustoming him to riding so that he will not become carsick on the day of a dog show. He should associate pleasure and attention with going in the car, van, or motor home. Take him where it is crowded: downtown, to the shops, everywhere you go that dogs are permitted. Make the expeditions fun for him by frequent petting and words of praise; do not just ignore him as you go about your errands.

Do not overly shelter your future show dog. Instinctively you may want to keep him at home where he is safe from germs or danger. This can be foolish on two counts. The first reason is that a puppy kept away from other dogs builds up no natural immunity against all the things with which he will come in contact at dog shows, so it is wiser actually to keep him well up to date on all protective shots and then let him become accustomed to being among dogs and dog owners. Also, a dog who never is among strange people, in strange places, or among strange dogs may grow up with a shyness or timidity of spirit that will cause you real problems as his show career draws near.

Ch. Jeffords Sherlock Holmes *(left)* and Ch. Jeffords Minute Man (uncropped) winning Best Non-Sporting Brace at Newton K.C. in August 1981. Owned by Mr. and Mrs. Marc Rosen, Scotland Yard Boston Terriers, Park Ridge, New Jersey.

Keep your show prospect's coat in immaculate condition with frequent grooming and daily brushing. When bathing is necessary, use a mild dog shampoo or whatever the breeder of your puppy may suggest. Several of the brand-name products do an excellent job. Be sure to rinse thoroughly so as not to risk skin irritation by traces of soap left behind, and protect against soap entering the eyes by a drop of castor oil in each before you lather up. Use warm water (be sure it is not uncomfortably hot or chillingly cold) and a good spray. Make certain you allow your dog to dry thoroughly in a warm, draft-free area (or outdoors, if it is warm and sunny) so that he doesn't catch cold. Then proceed to groom him to perfection.

Toenails should be watched and trimmed every few weeks. It is important not to permit nails to grow excessively long, as they will ruin the appearance of both the feet and pasterns.

A show dog's teeth must be kept clean and free of tartar. Hard dog biscuits can help toward this, but if tartar accumulates, see that it is removed promptly by your veterinarian. Bones for chewing are not suitable for show dogs as they tend to damage and wear down the tooth enamel.

Assuming that you will be handling the dog yourself, or even if he will be professionally handled, a few moments each day of dog show routine is important. Practice setting him up as you have seen the exhibitors do at the shows you've attended, and teach him to hold this position once you have him stacked to your satisfaction. Make the learning period pleasant by being firm but lavish in your praise when he responds correctly. Teach him to gait at your side at a moderate rate on a loose lead. When you have mastered the basic essentials at home, then hunt out and join a training class for future work. Training classes are sponsored by show-giving clubs in many areas, and their popularity is steadily increasing. If you have no other way of locating one, perhaps your veterinarian would know of one through some of his other clients; but if you are sufficiently aware of the dog show world to want a show dog, you will probably be personally acquainted with other people who will share information of this type with you.

Accustom your show dog to being in a crate (which you should be doing with a pet dog as well). He should relax in his crate at the shows "between times" for his own well being and safety.

MATCH SHOWS

Your show dog's initial experience in the ring should be in match show competition for several reasons. First, this type of event is intended as a learning experience for both the dog and the exhibitor. You will not feel embarrassed or out of place no matter how poorly your puppy may behave or how inept your attempts at handling may be, as you will find others there with the same type of problems. The important thing is that you get the puppy out and into a show ring where the two of you can practice together and learn the ropes.

Only on rare occasions is it necessary to make match show entries in advance, and even those with a pre-entry policy will usually accept entries at the door as well. Thus you need not plan several weeks ahead, as is the case with point shows, but can go when the mood strikes you. Also there is a vast difference in the cost, as match show entries only cost a few dollars while entry fees for the point shows may be over ten dollars, an amount none of us needs to waste until we have some idea of how the puppy will behave or how much more pre-show training is needed.

Match shows very frequently are judged by professional handlers who, in addition to making the awards, are happy to help new exhibitors with comments and advice on their puppies and their presentation of them. Avail yourself of all these opportunities before heading out to the sophisticated world of the point shows.

POINT SHOWS

As previously mentioned, entries for American Kennel Club point shows must be made in advance. This must be done on an official entry blank of the show-giving club. The entry must then be filed either personally or by mail with the show superintendent or the show secretary (if the event is being run by the club members alone and a superintendent has not been hired, this information will appear on the premium list) in time to reach its destination prior to the published closing date or filling of the quota. These entries must be made carefully, must be signed by the owner of the dog or the owner's agent (your professional handler), and must be accompanied by the entry fee; otherwise they will not be accepted. Remember that it is not when the entry leaves your hands that counts, but the date of arrival at its destination. If you are relying on the mails, which are not always dependable, get the entry off well before the deadline to avoid disappointment.

A dog must be entered at a dog show in the name of the actual owner at the time of the entry closing date of that specific show. If a registered dog has been acquired by a new owner, it must be entered in the name of the new owner in any show for which entries close after the date of acquirement, regardless of whether the new owner has or has not actually received the registration certificate indicating that the dog is recorded in his name. State on the entry form whether or not transfer application has been mailed to the American Kennel Club, and it goes without saying that the latter should be attended to promptly when you purchase a registered dog.

In filling out your entry blank, type, print, or write clearly, paying particular attention to the spelling of names, correct registration numbers, and so on. Also, if there is more than one variety in your breed, be sure to indicate into which category your dog is being entered.

The Puppy Class is for dogs or bitches who are six months of age and under twelve months and who are not champions. The age of a dog shall be calculated up to and inclusive of the first day of a show. For example, the first day a dog whelped on January 1st is eligible to compete in a Puppy Class at a show is July 1st of the same year; and he may continue to compete in Puppy Classes up to and including a show on December 31st of the same year, but he is *not* eligible to compete in a Puppy Class at a show held on or after January 1st of the following year.

The Puppy Class is the first one in which you should enter your puppy. In it a certain allowance will be made for the fact that they *are* puppies, thus an immature dog or one displaying less than perfect showmanship will be less severely penalized than, for instance, would be the case in Open. It is also quite likely that others in the class will be suffering from these problems, too. When you enter a puppy, be sure to check the classification with care, as some shows divide their Puppy Class into a 6-9 months old section and a 9-12 months old section.

The Novice Class is for dogs six months of age and over, whelped in the United States or Canada, who *prior to the official closing date for entries* have *not* won three first prizes in the Novice

The memorable bitch Ch. Payson's Miss Patricia G. G. winning Best American-bred in Show (an A.K.C. award of that time period) at Albany K.C. 1949 under the author. Eddie Campbell handling for owner, Charles D. Cline of California. G.G. was a big winner on the Coast, and piled up an enviable record of important successes.

Ch. Showbiz Rick O'Shay Romance with six of his "kids" in the Stud Dog Class at Pacific Coast Specialty under judge Raphael Schulte (far left). They all won blue ribbons in their classes that day. The two on the far right became champions.

Ch. Gentleman Jim Regardless with owner-handler Lillian Huddleston and judge Joseph Faigel, winning Best of Breed, then a Group 4th the same day. Arthur and Lillian Huddleston, Showbiz Bostons, Northridge, California.

Left: Ch. Regal Legacy Alexander's Fame, by Am. and Can. Ch. Simms Hi-hope Mr. Hobo ex Regal Legacy's Hyregards, taking Best of Winners at Alamance in 1984. Bred and owned by Jose F. Negron and Anthony A. Antolics, Alexandria, Virginia. *Right:* Am. and Can. Ch. Chahary Adonis Jovan, bred, owned, and handled by Mrs. Ira Smoluchowski, Chahary Kennels, Rockford, Illinois.

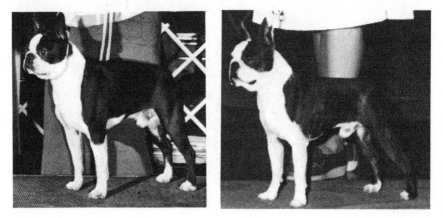

Class, any first prize at all in the Bred-by-Exhibitor, American-bred, or Open Classes, or one or more points toward championship. The provisions for this class are confusing to many people, which is probably the reason exhibitors do not enter in it more frequently. A dog may win any number of first prizes in the Puppy Class and still retain his eligibility for Novice. He may place second, third, or fourth not only in Novice on an unlimited number of occasions, but also in Bred-by-Exhibitor, American-bred and Open and still remain eligible for Novice. But he may no longer be shown in Novice when he has won three blue ribbons in that class, when he has won even one blue ribbon in either Bred-by-Exhibitor, American-bred, or Open, or when he has won a single championship point.

In determining whether or not a dog is eligible for the Novice Class, keep in mind the fact that previous wins are calculated according to the official published date for closing of entries, not by the date on which you may actually have made the entry. So if in the interim, between the time you made the entry and the official closing date, your dog makes a win causing him to become ineligible for Novice, change your class *immediately* to another for which he will be eligible, preferably either Bred-by-Exhibitor or American-bred. To do this, you must contact the show's superintendent or secretary, at first by telephone to save time and then in writing to confirm it. The Novice Class always seems to have the fewest entries of any class, and therefore it is a splendid "practice ground" for you and your young dog while you are getting the "feel" of being in the ring.

Bred-by-Exhibitor Class is for dogs whelped in the United States or, if individually registered in the American Kennel Club Stud Book, for dogs whelped in Canada who are six months of age or older, are not champions, and are owned wholly or in part by the person or by the spouse of the person who was the breeder or one of the breeders of record. Dogs entered in this class must be handled in the class by an owner or by a member of the immediate family of the owner. Members of an immediate family for this purpose are husband, wife, father, mother, son, daughter, brother, or sister. This is the class which is really the "breeders' showcase," and the one which breeders should enter with particular pride to show off their achievements.

The American-bred Class is for all dogs excepting champions, six months of age or older, who were whelped in the United States by reason of a mating which took place in the United States.

The Open Class is for any dog six months of age or older (this is the only restriction for this class). Dogs with championship points compete in it, dogs who are already champions are eligible to do so, dogs who are imported can be entered, and, of course, American-bred dogs compete in it. This class is, for some strange reason, the favorite of exhibitors who are "out to win." They rush to enter their pointed dogs in it, under the false impression that by doing so they assure themselves of greater attention from the judges. This really is not so, and some people feel that to enter in one of the less competitive classes, with a better chance of winning it and thus earning a second opportunity of gaining the judge's approval by returning to the ring in the Winners Class, can often be a more effective strategy.

One does not enter the Winners Class. One earns the right to compete in it by winning first prize in Puppy, Novice, Bred-by-Exhibitor, American-bred, or Open. No dog who has been defeated on the same day in one of these classes is eligible to compete for Winners, and every dog who has been a blue-ribbon winner in one of them and not defeated in another, should he have been entered in more than one class (as occasionally happens), *must* do so. Following the selection of the Winners Dog or the Winners Bitch, the dog or bitch receiving that award leaves the ring. Then the dog or bitch who placed second in that class, unless previously beaten by another dog or bitch in another class at the same show, re-enters the ring to compete against the remaining first-prize winners for Reserve. The latter award indicates that the dog or bitch selected for it is standing "in reserve" should the one who received Winners be disqualified or declared ineligible through any technicality when the awards are checked at the American Kennel Club. In that case, the one who placed Reserve is moved up to Winners, at the same time receiving the appropriate championship points.

Winners Dog and Winners Bitch are the awards which carry points toward championship with them. The points are based on the number of dogs or bitches actually in competition, and the points are scaled one through five, the latter being the greatest number available to any one dog or bitch at any one show. Three-, four-, or five-point wins are considered majors. In order to become a champion, a dog or bitch must have won two majors under two different judges, plus at least one point from a third judge, and the additional points necessary to bring the total to fifteen. When your dog has gained fifteen points as described above, a championship certificate will be issued to you, and your dog's name will be published in the champions of record list in the *Pure-Bred Dogs/American Kennel Gazette*, the official publication of the American Kennel Club.

The scale of championship points for each breed is worked out by the American Kennel Club and reviewed annually, at which time the number required in competition may be either changed (raised or lowered) or remain the same. The scale of championship points for all breeds is published annually in the May issue of the *Gazette*, and the current ratings for each breed within that area are published in every show catalog.

When a dog or bitch is adjudged Best of Winners, its championship points are, for that show, compiled on the basis of which sex had the greater number of points. If there are two points in dogs and four in bitches and the dog goes Best of Winners, then *both* the dog and the bitch are awarded an equal number of points, in this case four. Should the Winners Dog or the Winners Bitch go on to win Best of Breed or Best of Variety, additional points are accorded for the additional dogs and bitches defeated by so doing, provided, of course, that there were entries specifically for Best of Breed competition or Specials, as these specific entries are generally called.

If your dog or bitch takes Best of Opposite Sex after going Winners, points are credited according to the number of the same sex defeated in both the regular classes and Specials competition. If Best of Winners is also won, then whatever additional points for each of these awards are available will be credited. Many a one- or two-point win has grown into a major in this manner.

Moving further along, should your dog win its Variety Group from the classes (in other words, if it has taken either Winners Dog or Winners Bitch), you then receive points based on the greatest number of points awarded to any member of any breed included within that Group during that show's competition.

Should the day's winning also include Best in Show, the same rule of thumb applies, and your dog or bitch receives the highest number of points awarded to any other dog of any breed at that event.

Best of Breed competition consists of the Winners Dog and the Winners Bitch, who automatically compete on the strength of those awards, in addition to whatever dogs and bitches have been entered specifically for this class for which champions of record are eligible. Since July 1980, dogs who, according to their owner's records, have completed the requirements for a championship after the closing of entries for the show (but whose championships are unconfirmed) may be transferred from one of the regular classes to the Best of Breed competition, provided this transfer is made by the show superintendent or show secretary *prior to the start of any judging at the show.*

This has proved an extremely popular new rule, as under it a dog can finish on Saturday and then be transferred and compete as a Special on Sunday. It must be emphasized that *the change must be made prior to the start of any part of the day's judging, not for just your individual breed.*

In the United States, Best of Breed winners are entitled to compete in the Variety Group which includes them. This is not mandatory; it is a privilege which exhibitors value. (In Canada, Best of Breed winners *must* compete in the Variety Group or they lose any points already won.) The dogs winning *first* in each of the seven Variety Groups *must* compete for Best in Show. Missing the opportunity of taking your dog in for competition in its Group is foolish, as it is there where the general public is most likely to notice your breed and become interested in learning about it.

Non-regular classes are sometimes included at the all-breed shows, and they are almost invariably included at Specialty shows. These include Stud Dog Class and Brood Bitch Class, which are judged on the basis of the quality of the two offspring accompanying the sire or dam. The quality of the latter two is beside the point and should not be considered by the judge; it is the youngsters who count, and the quality of *both* are to be averaged to decide which sire or dam is the best and most consistent producer. Then there is the Brace Class (which, at all-breed shows, moves up to Best Brace in each Variety Group and then Best Brace in

Show) which is judged on the similarity and evenness of appearance of the two brace members. In other words, the two dogs should look like identical twins in size, color, and conformation and should move together almost as a single dog, one person handling with precision and ease. The same applies to the Team Class competition, except that four dogs are involved and, if necessary, two handlers.

The Veterans Class is for the older dogs, the minimum age of whom is seven years. This class is judged on the quality of the dogs, as the winner competes in Best of Breed competition and has, on a respectable number of occasions, been known to take that top award. So the point is *not* to pick out the oldest dog, as some judges seem to believe, but the best specimen of the breed, exactly as in the regular classes.

Then there are Sweepstakes and Futurity Stakes sponsored by many Specialty clubs, sometimes as part of their regular Specialty shows and sometimes as separate events on an entirely different occasion. The difference between the two stakes is that Sweepstakes entries usually include dogs from six to eighteen months of age with entries made at the same time as the others for the show, while for a Futurity the entries are bitches nominated when bred and the individual puppies entered at or shortly following their birth.

JUNIOR SHOWMANSHIP COMPETITION

If there is a youngster in your family between the ages of ten and sixteen, there is no better or more rewarding hobby than becoming an active participant in Junior Showmanship. This is a marvelous activity for young people. It teaches responsibility, good sportsmanship, the fun of competition where one's own skills are the deciding factor of success, proper care of a pet, and how to socialize with other young folks. Any youngster may experience the thrill of emerging from the ring a winner and the satisfaction of a good job well done.

Entry in Junior Showmanshiop Classes is open to any boy or girl who is at least ten years old and under seventeen years old on the day of the show. The Novice Junior Showmanship Class is open to youngsters who have not already won, at the time the entries close, three firsts in this class. Youngsters who have won three firsts in Novice may compete in the Open Junior Showmanship Class. Any junior handler who wins his third first-place award in Novice may participate in the Open Class at the same show, provided that the Open Class has at least one other junior handler entered and competing in it that day. The Novice and Open Classes may be divided into Junior and Senior Classes. Youngsters between the ages of ten and twelve, inclusively, are eligible for the Junior division; and youngsters between thirteen and seventeen, inclusively, are eligible for the Senior division.

Any of the foregoing classes may be separated into individual classes for boys and for girls. If such a division is made, it must be so indicated on the premium list. The premium list also indicates the prize for Best Junior Handler, if such a prize is being offered at the show. Any youngster who wins a first in any of the regular classes may enter the competition for this prize, provided the youngster has been undefeated in any other Junior Showmanship Class at that show.

Junior Showmanship Classes, unlike regular conformation classes in which the quality of the dog is judged, are judged solely on the skill and ability of the junior handling the dog. Which dog is best is not the point—it is which youngster does the best job with the dog that is under consideration. Eligibility requirements for the dog being shown in Junior Showmanship, and other detailed information, can be found in *Regulations for Junior Showmanship*, available from the American Kennel Club.

A junior who has a dog that he or she can enter in both Junior Showmanship and conformation classes has twice the opportunity for success and twice the opportunity to get into the ring and work with the dog, a combination which can lead to not only awards for expert handling, but also, if the dog is of sufficient quality, for making a conformation champion.

PRE-SHOW PREPARATIONS

Preparation of the items you will need as a dog show exhibitor should not be left until the last moment. They should be planned and arranged for at least several days in advance of the show in order for you to remain calm and relaxed as the countdown starts.

The importance of the crate has already been mentioned and should already be part of your equipment. Of equal importance is

Ch. Blazermin's Waltzing Matilda in Junior Showmanship with Jim and Pat Cronen's granddaughter, Jessica. Conn, handling and taking First Prize. Owned by Jim Cronen, Louisville, Kentucky.

Am. and Can. Ch. Dan Jee's I'm Suzi Too sets herself up in a beautiful natural show pose as she intently watches her owner-handler Honore Rosen. This is the way you want your Boston to look in the show ring!

Honore handling her Boston Terrier sets an excellent example of a trained, alert little dog in perfect show pose as she "baits" for the tempting morsel in her owner's hand. Note how well the dog is placed in both fore- and hind-quarters.

the grooming table, which very likely you have also already acquired for use at home. You should take it along with you to the shows, as your dog will need last minute touches before entering the ring. Should you have not yet made this purchase, folding tables with rubber tops are made specifically for this purpose and can be purchased at most dog shows, where concession booths with marvelous assortments of "doggy" necessities are to be found, or at your pet supplier. You will also need a sturdy tack box (also available at the dog show concessions) in which to carry your grooming tools and equipment. The latter should include: brushes; combs; scissors; nail clippers; whatever you use for last minute clean-up jobs; cotton swabs; first-aid equipment; and anything you are in the habit of using on the dog, including a leash or two of the type you prefer, some well-cooked and dried-out liver or any of the small packaged "dog treats" for use as bait in the ring, an atomizer in case you wish to dampen your dog's coat when you are preparing him for the ring, and so on. A large turkish towel to spread under the dog on the grooming table is also useful.

Take a large thermos or cooler of ice, the biggest one you can accommodate in your vehicle, for use by "man and beast." Take a jug of water (there are lightweight, inexpensive ones available at all sporting goods shops) and a water dish. If you plan to feed the dog at the show, or if you and the dog will be away from home more than one day, bring food for him from home so that he will have the type to which he is accustomed.

You may or may not have an exercise pen. While the shows do provide areas for exercise of the dogs, these are among the most likely places to have your dog come in contact with any illnesses which may be going around, and having a pen of your own for your dog's use is excellent protection. Such a pen comes in handy while you're travelling; since it is roomier than a crate, it becomes a comfortable place for your dog to relax and move around in, especially when you're at motels or rest stops. These pens are available at the show concession stands and come in a variety of heights and sizes. A set of "pooper scoopers" should also be part of your equipment, along with a package of plastic bags for cleaning up after your dog.

Bring along folding chairs for the members of your party, unless all of you are fond of standing, as these are almost never provided anymore by the clubs. Have your name stamped on the chairs so that there will be no doubt as to whom the chairs belong. Bring whatever you and your family enjoy for drinks or snacks in a picnic basket or cooler, as show food, in general, is expensive and usually not great. You should always have a pair of boots, a raincoat, and a rain hat with you (they should remain permanently in your vehicle if you plan to attend shows regularly), as well as a sweater, a warm coat, and a change of shoes. A smock or big cover-up apron will assure that you remain tidy as you prepare the dog for the ring. Your overnight case should include a small sewing kit for emergency repairs, bandaids, headache and indigestion remedies, and any personal products or medications you normally use.

In your car you should always carry maps of the area where you are headed and an assortment of motel directories. Generally speaking, Holiday Inns have been found to be the nicest about taking dogs. Ramadas and Howard Johnsons generally do so cheerfully (with a few exceptions). Best Western generally frowns on pets (not always, but often enough to make it necessary to find out which do). Some of the smaller chains welcome pets; the majority of privately owned motels do not.

Have everything prepared the night before the show to expedite your departure. Be sure that the dog's identification and your judging program and other show information are in your purse or briefcase. If you are taking sandwiches, have them ready. Anything that goes into the car the night before the show will be one thing less to remember in the morning. Decide upon what you will wear and have it out and ready. If there is any question in your mind about what to wear, try on the possibilities before the day of the show; don't risk feeling you may want to change when you see yourself dressed a few moments prior to departure time!

In planning your outfit, make it something simple that will not detract from your dog. Remember that a dark dog silhouettes attractively against a light background and vice-versa. Sport clothes always seem to look best at dog shows, preferably conservative in type and not overly "loud" as you do not want to detract from your dog, who should be the focus of interest at this point. What you wear on your feet is important. Many types of flooring can be hazardously slippery, as can wet grass. Make it a habit to wear rubber soles and low or flat heels in the ring for your own safety, especially if you are showing a dog that likes to move out smartly.

Your final step in pre-show preparation is to leave yourself plenty of time to reach the show that morning. Traffic can get amazingly heavy as one nears the immediate area of the show, finding a parking place can be difficult, and other delays may occur. You'll be in better humor to enjoy the day if your trip to the show is not fraught with panic over fear of not arriving in time!

ENJOYING THE DOG SHOW

From the moment of your arrival at the show until after your dog has been judged, keep foremost in your mind the fact that he is your reason for being there and that he should therefore be the center of your attention. Arrive early enough to have time for those last-minute touches that can make a great difference when he enters the ring. Be sure that he has ample time to exercise and that he attends to personal matters. A dog arriving in the ring and immediately using it as an exercise pen hardly makes a favorable impression on the judge.

When you reach ringside, ask the steward for your arm-card and anchor it firmly into place on your arm. Make sure that you are where you should be when your class is called. The fact that you have picked up your arm-card does not guarantee, as some seem to think, that the judge will wait for you. The judge has a full schedule which he wishes to complete on time. Even though you may be nervous, assume an air of calm self-confidence. Remember that this is a hobby to be enjoyed, so approach it in that state of mind. The dog will do better, too, as he will be quick to reflect your attitude.

Always show your dog with an air of pride. If you make mistakes in presenting him, don't worry about it. Next time you will do better. Do not permit the presence of more experienced exhibitors to intimidate you. After all, they, too, once were newcomers.

The judging routine usually starts when the judge asks that the dogs be gaited in a circle around the ring. During this period the judge is watching each dog as it moves, noting style, topline, reach and drive, head and tail carriage, and general balance. Keep your mind and your eye on your dog, moving him at his most becoming gait and keeping your place in line without coming too close to the exhibitor ahead of you. Always keep your dog on the inside of the circle, between yourself and the judge, so that the judge's view of the dog is unobstructed.

Calmly pose the dog when requested to set up for examination. If you are at the head of the line and many dogs are in the class, go all the way to the end of the ring before starting to stack the dog, leaving sufficient space for those behind you to line theirs up as well, as requested by the judge. If you are not at the head of the line but between other exhibitors, leave sufficient space ahead of your dog for the judge to examine him. The dogs should be spaced so that the judge is able to move among them to see them from all angles. In practicing to "set up" or "stack" your dog for the judge's examination, bear in mind the importance of doing so quickly and with dexterity. The judge has a schedule to meet and only a few moments in which to evaluate each dog. You will immeasurably help yours to make a favorable impression if you are able to "get it all together" in a minimum amount of time. Practice at home before a mirror can be a great help toward bringing this about, facing the dog so that you see him from the same side that the judge will and working to make him look right in the shortest length of time.

Listen carefully as the judge describes the manner in which the dog is to be gaited, whether it is straight down and straight back; down the ring, across, and back; or in a triangle. The latter has become the most popular pattern with the majority of judges. "In a triangle" means the dog should move down the outer side of the ring to the first corner, across that end of the ring to the second corner, and then back to the judge from the second corner, using the center of the ring in a diagonal line. Please learn to do this pattern without breaking at each corner to twirl the dog around you, a senseless maneuver that has been noticed on occasion. Judges like to see the dog in an uninterrupted triangle, as they are thus able to get a better idea of the dog's gait.

It is impossible to overemphasize that the gait at which you move your dog is tremendously important and considerable study and thought should be given to the matter. At home, have someone move the dog for you at different speeds so that you can tell

The famous sire, Ch. B.B.'s Dudes Little Hobo, son of Ch. Eanes Dude The Little Rebel ex Ch. Toy Town's High Stepping Lana, was bred by Elaine Newbecker and is owned by Neva Stewart of Fairfax, Virginia. An outstanding stud dog, with noted champion sons and daughters.

which shows him off to best advantage. The most becoming action almost invariably is seen at a moderate gait, head up and topline holding. Do not gallop your dog around the ring or hurry him into a speed atypical of his breed. Nothing being rushed appears at its best; give your dog a chance to move along at his (and the breed's) natural gait. For a dog's action to be judged accurately, that dog should move with strength and power, but not excessive speed, holding a straight line as he goes to and from the judge.

As you bring the dog back to the judge, stop him a few feet away and be sure that he is standing in a becoming position. Bait him to show the judge an alert expression, using whatever tasty morsel he has been trained to expect for this purpose or, if that works better for you, use a small squeak-toy in your hand. A reminder, please, to those using liver or treats. Take them with you when you leave the ring. Do not just drop them on the ground where they will be found by another dog.

When the awards have been made, accept yours graciously, no matter how you actually may feel about it. What's done is done, and arguing with a judge or stomping out of the ring is useless and a reflection on your sportsmanship. Be courteous, congratulate the winner if your dog was defeated, and try not to show your disappointment. By the same token, please be a gracious winner; this, surprisingly, sometimes seems to be still more difficult.

Ch. R. T.'s Cricket of Tru-Mark, C.D., taking points towards her title at Rock Creek 1984 under judge William Haupt. Owned by Dorothy Truman, Rockbridge Baths, Virginia.

Chapter 12

Your Boston Terrier and Obedience

For its own protection and safety, every dog should be taught, at the very least, to recognize and obey the commands "Come," "Heel," "Down," "Sit," and "Stay." Doing so at some time might save the dog's life and in less extreme circumstances will certainly make him a better behaved, more pleasant member of society. If you are patient and enjoy working with your dog, study some of the excellent books available on the subject of obedience and then teach your canine friend these basic manners. If you need the stimulus of working with a group, find out where obedience training classes are held (usually your veterinarian, your dog's breeder, or a dog-owning friend can tell you) and you and your dog can join up. Alternatively, you could let someone else do the training by sending the dog to class, but this is not very rewarding because you lose the opportunity of working with your dog and the pleasure of the rapport thus established.

If you are going to do it yourself, there are some basic rules which you should follow. You must remain calm and confident in attitude. Never lose your temper and frighten or punish your dog unjustly. Be quick and lavish with praise each time a command is correctly followed. Make it fun for the dog and he will be eager to please you by responding correctly. Repetition is the keynote, but it should not be continued without recess to the point of tedium. Limit the training sessions to ten- or fifteen-minute periods at a time.

Formal obedience training can be followed, and very frequently is, by entering the dog in obedience competition to work toward an obedience degree, or several of them, depending on the dog's aptitude and your own enjoyment. Obedience trials are held in conjunction with the majority of all-breed conformation dog shows, with Specialty shows, and frequently as separate Specialty events. If you are working alone with your dog, a list of trial dates might be obtained from your dog's veterinarian, your dog breeder, or a dog-owning friend; the AKC *Gazette* lists shows and trials to be scheduled in the coming months; and if you are a member of a training class, you will find the information readily available.

The goals for which one works in the formal AKC Member or Licensed Trials are the following titles: Companion Dog (C.D.), Companion Dog Excellent (C.D.X.), and Utility Dog (U.D.). These degrees are earned by receiving three "legs," or qualifying scores, at each level of competition. The degrees must be earned in order, with one completed prior to starting work on the next. For example, a dog must have earned C.D. prior to starting work on C.D.X.; then C.D.X. must be completed before U.D. work begins. The ultimate title attainable in obedience work is Obedience Trial Champion (O.T.Ch.)

When you see the letters C.D. following a dog's name, you will know that this dog has satisfactorily completed the following exercises: heel on leash and figure eight, heel free, stand for examination, recall, long sit, and long down. C.D.X. means that tests have been passed on all of those just mentioned plus heel free and figure eight, drop on recall, retrieve on flat, retrieve over high jump, broad jump, long sit, and long down. U.D. indicates that the dog has additionally passed tests in scent discrimination (leather article), scent discrimination (metal article), signal exercise, directed retrieve, directed jumping, and group stand for examination. The letters O.T.Ch. are the abbreviation for the only obedience title

Kathryn the Great of Bar None, U.D., owned, trained, and shown by Robert L. Breum, Omaha, Nebraska, who at one time owned two U.D. Boston Terriers together.

which precedes rather than follows a dog's name. To gain an obedience trial championship, a dog who already holds a Utility Dog degree must win a total of one hundred points and must win three firsts, under three different judges, in Utility and Open B Classes.

There is also a Tracking Dog title (T.D.) which can be earned at tracking trials. In order to pass the tracking tests the dog must follow the trail of a stranger along a path on which the trail was laid between thirty minutes and two hours previously. Along this track there must be more than two right-angle turns, at least two of which are well out in the open where no fences or other boundaries exist for the guidance of the dog or the handler. The dog wears a harness and is connected to the handler by a lead twenty to forty feet in length. Inconspicuously dropped at the end of the track is an article to be retrieved, usually a glove or wallet, which the dog is expected to locate and the handler to pick up. The letters T.D.X. are the abbreviation for Tracking Dog Excellent, a more difficult version of the Tracking Dog test with a longer track and more turns to be worked through.

Can. Ch. Flo-ra's
Dani Boy of Robb
Isle, C.D., owned by
Bob and Dianne
Lowes, Wyebridge,
Ontario, Canada.

SOME BOSTON TERRIERS IN OBEDIENCE

For some reason, unexplainable to me, in the minds of the public Boston Terriers are seldom thought of as dogs who might attain success in obedience competition, which could not be further from the truth, and is an unwarranted injustice to this splendid breed. Actually, the intelligence, alertness, and desire to please of a Boston Terrier equips the breed extremely well, with the result that when given the opportunity, Boston Terriers have distinguished themselves admirably in this area.

A fancier who has long appreciated the talents of the Boston Terrier in obedience is Robert L. Breum of Omaha, Nebraska, who has shown a number of them to C.D. degrees, some who have gone on to C.D.X., and even at least two of his who have attained Utility Dog honors.

Miss Ami of Bar None, owned by Mr. Breum, was the first Boston to earn the Companion Dog degree for him, and thus bring about his continued involvement with obedience work.

Another of Robert Breum's obedience "stars," Miss Janie of Bar None, Utility Dog, was highest scoring Boston Terrier in obedience for 1967, during which year she accumulated three times as many points as did the closest runner up. In 1964 she was awarded the Dog World Award of Canine Distinction for achieving her Companion Dog Degree in three consecutive trials with scores of 195 or higher. Her best scores, it is interesting to note, were achieved in Open work where, in February 1968, she tied for Highest Scoring Dog in Trial at St. Joseph Kennel Club. The first time she competed in Utility she scored 197 1/2 out of a possible 200!

Over a four year period, Janie was shown about 80 times, at trials only within a reasonable distance from home. She was in the ribbons a good 50% of the time, with her wins almost evenly distributed between first to fourth place.

Both Ami and Janie came from Kathryn Schuett's Bar None Kennels. Janie was by Champion Iowana's Royalty Command and a granddaughter of Champion Grant's Royal Command. She was a half sister to the very famous Best of Breed winning show bitch Champion Iowana's Fancy Flair owned by Loretta Dunham.

Then came Kathryn the Great of Bar None, U.D., who was the foremost (and the first) Obedience Boston Terrier for 1971. This talented little Boston had started life as an amazingly tiny puppy whose dam refused to mother her. The Breums decided on sight that she had been intended for them, took her home, and made their oven into an incubator and provided nourishment for her at first with an eye dropper, then as she gained in size and strength, with a baby bottle. A bout with tonsilitis and a bout with pneumonia both left her undaunted, as did an especially severe winter. She matured into a very excellent Boston Terrier with a most gorgeous head, but still remained below average size.

Katy thought obedience had been created especially for her. She loved every moment of it, her only problem having been in doing the "retrieve" as, no matter what glove was indicated for her to pick up, she always went for the one in the center. The first two Utility legs posed no problems. This finally was overcome with a re-training course eliminating the middle glove. Eventually Katie got the idea, and all was well.

Dorothy Truman, of Tru-Mark Bostons, is another breeder of

bench champion Bostons who is also very obedience-oriented. From her kennel at Rockbridge Baths, Virginia, have come some distinguished C.D. winners, and she continues currently proving the talents of the Boston Terrier in the obedience rings.

The two breeds owned by Mrs. Truman are Boston Terriers and German Shepherd Dogs, to which fact she adds the comment, "but if I could only have one dog it would be a Boston." Bostons were the breed she grew up with as a child and the first she acquired following her marriage.

The one now known as Champion Clasen's Cherub, C.D., came from Harry Clasen's famed kennel during 1976 and, as that was her principal interest in dog activities at the time, Mrs. Truman promptly started her in obedience. This daughter of the noted sire, Champion Toby Junior II, took to it rather like a duck does to water, quickly completing her C.D. degree in three consecutive shows with good scores. Following this, Mrs. Truman added a German Shepherd to the family, and Cindy's career was put on a back burner temporarily. Starting out later in Open, and knowing full well how to perform the entire series of exercises, Cindy always managed to miss one thing or another during the trials, almost as though in retaliation for having been cast aside after doing so well with her earlier degree. Considering the intelligence of Boston Terriers, this does not seem at all hard to believe!

Cindy was bred twice, and the only three of her puppies ever shown became champions. Mrs. Truman kept one of the puppies from her second litter: she finished her bench championship at nine months and then, true to the tradition of "like mother, like daughter" added her obedience degree on October 27, 1985, thus becoming Champion R.T.'s Cricket of Tru-Mark.

THERAPY BOSTON TERRIERS

There is a beautiful little Boston Terrier named Our Bambi Dear, C.D., who is now ten years old. This is a Boston of very special accomplishments, for in addition to having earned a Companion Dog Degree in the obedience field, Bambi works as a Therapy Dog and is a member of Therapy Dogs International.

Bambi's owner, Lyda McFarland of Menands, New York, explains that T.D.I. members wear a special yellow identification tag on their collars, and are obedience trained.

Littermates going Best of Winners (the Winners Bitch) and Winners Dog. These two are Ch. R.T.'s Cricket of Tru-Mark, C.D. owned by Dorothy Truman, Rockbridge Baths, Virginia; and Ch. Buster of Tru-Mark owned by Robert Marvel, Lancaster, Pennsylvania. Bred by Mrs. Truman, these two are offspring of her Ch. Clasen's Cherub, C.D. and sired by Ch. Mi-Toi's Topper's Chip N Doll.

The idea behind this group is to provide well behaved and lovable dogs to visit all sorts of homes and hospitals for the purpose of brightening an hour or two each visit for the patients there. Bambi and Lyda are members of the Albany Obedience Club and belong to that group's "Canine Company" which has visited nursing homes, veterans hospitals, schools, and homes for the retarded. The performances are always followed by a "petting session" which Lyda describes as a "special time for loving and sharing love which brings out the best in our dogs as well as ourselves."

Bambi, whose photograph appears in the 1983 edition of *Who's Who in Boston Terriers* published by the Boston Terrier Club of Maryland, Inc., was bred by Ruth and Otto Dube, famous Boston Terrier fanciers over many years, from Albany, New York. He is a son of Champion Dube's Tops Again ex Dube's Tops Again Star Baby. He was born in April 1975.

Top: Ch. Talone's Topper-N-Tina with two offspring, Ch. Talone's Tisket-N-Tasket *(left)* and Ch. Talone's Tried-N-True *(right)*. Linebred from TNT bloodlines. Owned by John and Nancy Talone, Knoxville, Tennessee.

Chapter 13

Breeding Your Boston Terrier

The first responsibility of any person breeding dogs is to do so with care, forethought, and deliberation. It is inexcusable to breed more litters than you need to carry on your show program or to perpetuate your bloodlines. A responsible breeder should not cause a litter to be born without definite plans for the safe and happy disposition of the puppies.

A responsible dog breeder makes absolutely certain, so far as is humanly possible, that the home to which one of his puppies will go is a good home, one that offers proper care and an enthusiastic owner. To be admired are those breeders who insist on visiting (although doing so is not always feasible) the prospective owners of their puppies to see if they have suitable facilities for keeping a dog, to find out if they understand the responsibility involved, and to make certain if all members of the household are in accord regarding the desirability of owning one. All breeders should carefully check out the credentials of prospective purchasers to be sure that the puppy is being placed in responsible hands.

No breeder ever wants a puppy or grown dog he has raised to wind up in an animal shelter, in an experimental laboratory, or as a victim of a speeding car. While complete control of such a situation may be impossible, it is important to make every effort to turn over dogs to responsible people. When selling a puppy, it is

255

a good idea to do so with the understanding that should it become necessary to place the dog in other hands, the purchaser will first contact you, the breeder. You may want to help in some way, possibly by buying or taking back the dog or placing it elsewhere. It is not fair to just sell puppies and then never again give a thought to their welfare. Family problems arise, people may be forced to move where dogs are prohibited, or people just plain grow bored with a dog and its care. Thus the dog becomes a victim. You, as the dog's breeder, should concern yourself with the welfare of each of your dogs and see to it that the dog remains in good hands.

The final obligation every dog owner shares, be there just one dog or an entire kennel involved, is that of making detailed, explicit plans for the future of these dearly loved animals in the event of the owner's death. Far too many people are apt to procrastinate and leave this very important matter unattended to, feeling that everything will work out or that "someone will see to them." The latter is not too likely, at least not to the benefit of the dogs, unless you have done some advance planning which will assure their future well-being.

Life is filled with the unexpected, and even the youngest, healthiest, most robust of us may be the victim of a fatal accident or sudden illness. The fate of your dogs, so entirely in your hands, should never be left to chance. If you have not already done so, please get together with your lawyer and set up a clause in your will specifying what you want done with each of your dogs, to whom they will be entrusted (after first making absolutely certain that the person selected is willing and able to assume the responsibility), and telling the locations of all registration papers, pedigrees, and kennel records. Just think of the possibilities which might happen otherwise! If there is another family member who shares your love of the dogs, that is good and you have less to worry about. But if your heirs are not dog-oriented, they will hardly know how to proceed or how to cope with the dogs themselves, and they may wind up disposing of or caring for your dogs in a manner that would break your heart were you around to know about it.

It is advisable to have in your will specific instructions concerning each of your dogs. A friend, also a dog person who regards his or her own dogs with the same concern and esteem as you do, may agree to take over their care until they can be placed accordingly and will make certain that all will work out as you have planned. This person's name and phone number can be prominently displayed in your van or car and in your wallet. Your lawyer can be made aware of this fact. This can be spelled out in your will. The friend can have a signed check of yours to be used in case of an emergency or accident when you are traveling with the dogs; this check can be used to cover his or her expense to come and take over the care of your dogs should anything happen to make it impossible for you to do so. This is the least any dog owner should do in preparation for the time their dogs suddenly find themselves alone. There have been so many sad cases of dogs unprovided for by their loving owners, left to heirs who couldn't care less and who disposed of them in any way at all to get rid of them, or left to heirs who kept and neglected them under the misguided idea that they were providing them "a fine home with lots of freedom." These misfortunes must be prevented from befalling your own dogs who have meant so much you!

An earlier chapter discussed selection of a bitch you plan to use for breeding. In making this important purchase, you will be choosing a bitch whom you hope will become the foundation of your kennel. Thus she must be of the finest producing bloodlines, excellent in temperament, of good type, and free of major faults or unsoundness. If you are offered a "bargain" brood bitch, be wary, as for this purchase you should not settle for less than the best and the price will be in accordance with the quality.

Conscientious breeders feel quite strongly that the only possible reason for producing puppies is the ambition to improve and uphold quality and temperament within the breed—definitely *not* because one hopes to make a quick cash profit on a mediocre litter, which never seems to work out that way in the long run and which accomplishes little beyond perhaps adding to the nation's heartbreaking number of unwanted canines. The only reason ever for breeding a litter is, with conscientious people, a desire to improve the quality of dogs in their own kennel or, as pet owners, to add to the number of dogs they themselves own with a puppy or two from their present favorites. In either case breeding should not take place unless one definitely has prospective owners for as

Joe Glaser's great bitch, Ch. Fritzie Regards of Pequa, winning a hotly contested Non-Sporting Group from the author in 1951. A gorgeous daughter of Ch. Regards Regardless of Pequa ex Illonas Pal, she was bred by Helen Fritz and born September 22, 1949. Handled by Albert Rosenbloom.

many puppies as the litter may contain, lest you find yourself with several fast-growing young dogs and no homes in which to place them.

THE BROOD BITCH

Bitches should not be mated earlier than their second season, by which time they should be from fifteen to eighteen months old. Many breeders prefer to wait and first finish the championships of their show bitches before breeding them, as pregnancy can be a disaster to a show coat and getting the bitch back in shape again takes time. When you have decided what will be the proper time, start watching at least several months ahead for what you feel would be the perfect mate to best complement your bitch's quality and bloodlines. Subscribe to the magazines which feature your breed exclusively and to some which cover all breeds in order to familiarize yourself with outstanding stud dogs in areas other than your own, for there is no necessity nowadays to limit your choice to a local dog unless you truly like him and feel that he is the most suitable. It is quite usual to ship a bitch to a stud dog a distance away, and this generally works out with no ill effects. The important thing is that you need a stud dog strong in those features where your bitch is weak or lacking, a dog whose bloodlines are compatible with hers. Compare the background of both your bitch and the stud dog under consideration, paying particular attention to the quality of the puppies from bitches with backgrounds similar to your bitch's. If the puppies have been of the type and quality you admire, then this dog would seem a sensible choice for yours, too.

Stud fees may be a few hundred dollars, sometimes even more under special situations for a particularly successful sire. It is money well spent, however. *Do not* ever breed to a dog because he is less expensive than the others unless you honestly believe that he can sire the kind of puppies who will be a credit to your kennel and your breed.

Contacting the owners of the stud dogs you find interesting will bring you pedigrees and pictures which you can then study in relation to your bitch's pedigree and conformation. Discuss your plans with other breeders who are knowledgeable (including the one who bred your own bitch). You may not always receive an entirely unbiased opinion (particularly if the person giving it also has

Ch. Dynamic Doll, Ch. Carry On Command ex Iowana's Velvet Belle II, in February 1968. Doll's first important win was at the Parent Club in Boston, where she took Winners bitch, Best of Winners, and Best of Opposite Sex under Mrs. David Dancer, repeating these wins the following week in Chicago, where she was sold to Ray A. Kibler of Maine. She went on to win the New York Specialty and the Chicago Specialty, and many other show ring successes. Pictured at the N.Y. Specialty handled by Albert Rosenbloom. Photo courtesy of Leonard L. Myers.

an available stud dog), but one learns by discussion so listen to what they say, consider their opinions, and then you may be better qualified to form your own opinion.

As soon as you have made a choice, phone the owner of the stud dog you wish to use to find out if this will be agreeable. You will be asked about the bitch's health, soundness, temperament, and freedom from serious faults. A copy of her pedigree may be requested, as might a picture of her. A discussion of her background over the telephone may be sufficient to assure the stud's owner that she is suitable for the stud dog and that she is of type, breeding, and quality herself, capable of producing the kind of puppies for which the stud is noted. The owner of a top-quality stud is often extremely selective in the bitches permitted to be bred to his dog, in an effort to keep the standard of his puppies high. The owner of a stud dog may require that the bitch be tested for brucellosis, which should be attended to not more than a month previous to the breeding.

Check out which airport will be most convenient for the person meeting and returning the bitch, if she is to be shipped, and also what airlines use that airport. You will find that the airlines are also apt to have special requirements concerning acceptance of animals for shipping. These include weather limitations and types of crates which are acceptable. The weather limits have to do with extreme heat and extreme cold at the point of destination, as some airlines will not fly dogs into temperatures above or below certain levels, fearing for their safety. The crate problem is a simple one, since, if your own crate is not suitable, most of the airlines have specially designed crates available for purchase at a fair and moderate price. It is a good plan to purchase one of these if you intend to be shipping dogs with any sort of frequency. They are made of fiberglass and are the safest type to use for shipping.

Normally you must notify the airline several days in advance to make a reservation, as they are able to accommodate only a certain number of dogs on each flight. Plan on shipping the bitch on about her eighth or ninth day of season, but be careful to avoid shipping her on a weekend when schedules often vary and freight offices are apt to be closed. Whenever you can, ship your bitch on a direct flight. Changing planes always carries a certain amount of risk of a dog being overlooked or wrongly routed at the middle

Ch. Showbiz Rick O'Shay Romance winning the Pacific Coast Specialty Show October 23, 1966 under judge Vincent Perry, going through from the classes to Winners dog, Best of Winners and Best in Show. Handled by Lillian Huddleston for herself and husband Arthur, Northridge, California.

No. 1 Boston Terrier Bitch in the Nation was quickly achieved by this remarkable Ch. Milady Deacon of Boston as she swept through to multiple Bests in Show and Non-Sporting Group awards during her exciting show career handled by Jerry Rigden for Dr. and Mrs. Robert Ritchey, Canal Fulton, Ohio. By Ch. Good Time Jody T. Brown ex Good Time Teddy J Brown, she was bred by Thomas L. Enwright. Pictured here winning the Group at Columbiana in 1982 judged by the author.

stop, so avoid this danger if at all possible. The bitch must be accompanied by a health certificate which you must obtain from your veterinarian before taking her to the airport. Usually it will be necessary to have the bitch at the airport about two hours prior to flight time. Before finalizing arrangements, find out from the stud's owner at what time of day it will be most convenient to have the bitch picked up promptly upon arrival.

It is simpler if you can plan to bring the bitch to the stud dog yourself. Some people feel that the trauma of the flight may cause the bitch to not conceive; and, of course, undeniably there is a slight risk in shipping which can be avoided if you are able to drive the bitch to her destination. Be sure to leave yourself sufficient time to assure your arrival at the right time for her for breeding (normally the tenth to fourteenth day following the first signs of color); and remember that if you want the bitch bred twice, you should allow a day to elapse between the two matings. Do not expect the stud's owner to house you while you are there. Locate a nearby motel that takes dogs and make that your headquarters.

Just prior to the time your bitch is due in season, you should take her to visit your veterinarian. She should be checked for worms and should receive all the booster shots for which she is due plus one for parvovirus, unless she has had the latter shot fairly recently. The brucellosis test can also be done then, and the health certificate can be obtained for shipping if she is to travel by air. Should the bitch be at all overweight, now is the time to get the surplus off. She should be in good condition, neither underweight nor overweight, at the time of breeding.

The moment you notice the swelling of the vulva, for which you should be checking daily as the time for her season approaches, and the appearance of color, immediately contact the stud's owner and settle on the day for shipping or make the appointment for your arrival with the bitch for breeding. If you are shipping the bitch, the stud fee check should be mailed immediately, leaving ample time for it to have been received when the bitch arrives and the mating takes place. Be sure to call the airline, making her reservation at that time, too.

Do not feed the bitch within a few hours before shipping her. Be certain that she has had a drink of water and been well exercised before closing her in the crate. Several layers of newspapers, topped with some shredded newspaper, make a good bed and can be discarded when she arrives at her destination; these can be replaced with fresh newspapers for her return home. Remember that the bitch should be brought to the airport about two hours before flight time, as sometimes the airlines refuse to accept late arrivals.

If you are taking your bitch by car, be certain that you will arrive at a reasonable time of day. Do not appear late in the evening. If your arrival in town is not until late, get a good night's sleep at your motel and contact the stud's owner first thing in the morning. If possible, leave children and relatives at home, as they will only be in the way and perhaps unwelcome by the stud's owner. Most stud dog owners prefer not to have any unnecessary people on hand during the actual mating.

After the breeding has taken place, if you wish to sit and visit for awhile and the stud's owner has the time, return the bitch to her crate in your car (first ascertaining, of course, that the temperature is comfortable for her and that there is proper ventilation). She should not be permitted to urinate for at least one hour following the breeding. This is the time when you get the business part of the transaction attended to. Pay the stud fee, upon which you should receive your breeding certificate and, if you do not already have it, a copy of the stud dog's pedigree. The owner of the stud dog does not sign or furnish a litter registration application until the puppies have been born.

Upon your return home, you can settle down and plan in happy anticipation a wonderful litter of puppies. A word of caution! Remember that although she has been bred, your bitch is still an interesting target for all male dogs, so guard her carefully for the next week or until you are absolutely certain that her season has entirely ended. This would be no time to have any unfortunate incident with another dog.

THE STUD DOG

Choosing the best stud dog to complement your bitch is often very difficult. The two principal factors to be considered should be the stud's conformation and his pedigree. Conformation is fairly obvious; you want a dog that is typical of the breed in the words of the Standard of perfection. Understanding pedigrees is a bit more subtle since the pedigree lists the ancestry of the dog and

The seven-year-old veteran, Ch. Williams Daddies Bigboy Beau, was winner of the Veterans' Class at the Boston Terrier Club of Miami Specialty in 1985. The sire, grandsire, and great grandsire of champions, he is the foundation dog at Startime Boston Terriers, Mrs. Yvette Williams Gulledge, Fort Myers, Florida.

involves individuals and bloodlines with which you may not be entirely familiar.

To a novice in the breed, then, the correct interpretation of a pedigree may at first be difficult to grasp. Study the pictures and text of this book and you will find many names of important bloodlines and members of the breed. Also make an effort to discuss the various dogs behind the proposed stud with some of the more experienced breeders, starting with the breeder of your own bitch. Frequently these folks will be personally familiar with many of the dogs in question, will be able to offer opinions of them, and may have access to additional pictures which you would benefit by seeing. It is very important that the stud's pedigree be harmonious with that of the bitch you plan on breeding to him. Do not rush out and breed to the latest winner with no thought of whether or not he can produce true quality. By no means are all great show dogs great producers. It is the producing record of the dog in question and the dogs and bitches from which he has come that should be the basis on which you make your choice.

Breeding dogs is never a money-making operation. By the time you pay a stud fee, care for the bitch during pregnancy, whelp the litter, and rear the puppies through their early shots, worming, and so on, you will be fortunate to break even financially once the puppies have been sold. Your chances of doing this are greater if you are breeding for a show-quality litter which will bring you higher prices, as the pups are sold as show prospects. Therefore, your wisest investment is to use the best dog available for your bitch regardless of the cost; then you should wind up with more valuable puppies. Remember that it is equally costly to raise mediocre puppies as it is top ones, and your chances of financial return are better on the latter. To breed to the most excellent, most suitable stud dog you can find is the only sensible thing to do, and it is poor economy to quibble over the amount you are paying in a stud fee.

It will be your decision which course you decide to follow when you breed your bitch, as there are three options: linebreeding, inbreeding, and outcrossing. Each of these methods has its supporters and its detractors! Linebreeding is breeding a bitch to a dog belonging originally to the same canine family, being descended from the same ancestors, such as half brother to half sister, grand-sire to granddaughter, niece to uncle (and vice-versa) or cousin to cousin. Inbreeding is breeding father to daughter, mother to son, or full brother to sister. Outcross breeding is breeding a dog and a bitch with no or only a few mutual ancestors.

Linebreeding is probably the safest course, and the one most likely to bring results, for the novice breeder. The more sophisti-cated inbreeding should be left to the experienced, longtime breeders who throroughly know and understand the risks and the possibilities involved with a particular line. It is usually done in an effort to intensify some ideal feature in that strain. Outcrossing is the reverse of inbreeding, an effort to introduce improvement in a specific feature needing correction, such as a shorter back, better movement, more correct head or coat, and so on.

It is the serious breeder's ambition to develop a strain or blood-line of their own, one strong in qualities for which their dogs will become distinguished. However, it must be realized that this will involve time, patience, and at least several generations before the achievement can be claimed. The safest way to embark on this plan, as previously mentioned, is by the selection and breeding of one or two bitches, the best you can buy and from top-producing kennels. In the beginning you do *not* really have to own a stud dog. In the long run it is less expensive and sounder judgement to pay a stud fee when you are ready to breed a bitch than to pur-chase a stud dog and feed him all year; a stud dog does not win any popularity contests with owners of bitches to be bred until he becomes a champion, has been successfully Specialed for a while, and has been at least moderately advertised, all of which adds up to quite a healthy expenditure.

The wisest course for the inexperienced breeder just starting out in dogs is as outlined above. Keep the best bitch puppy from the first several litters. After that you may wish to consider keep-ing your own stud dog, if there has been a particularly handsome male in one of your litters that you feel has great potential or if you know where there is one available that you are interested in, with the feeling that he would work in nicely with the breeding program on which you have embarked. By this time, with several litters already born, your eye should have developed to a point en-abling you to make a wise choice, either from one of your own litters or from among dogs you have seen that appear suitable.

The greatest care should be taken in the selection of your own stud dog. He must be of true type and highest quality as he may be responsible for siring many puppies each year, and he should come from a line of excellent dogs on both sides of his pedigree which themselves are, and which are descended from, successful producers. This dog should have no glaring faults in conformation; he should be of such quality that he can hold his own in keenest competition within his breed. He should be in good health, be virile and be a keen stud dog, a proven sire able to transmit his correct qualities to his puppies. Need one say that such a dog will be enormously expensive unless you have the good fortune to produce him in one of your own litters? To buy and use a lesser stud dog, however, is downgrading your breeding program unnecessarily since there are so many dogs fitting the description of a fine stud whose services can be used on payment of a stud fee.

You should *never* breed to an unsound dog or one with any serious disqualifying faults according to the breed's standard. Not all champions by any means pass along their best features; and by the same token, occasionally you will find a great one who can pass along his best features but never gained his championship title due to some unusual circumstances. The information you need about a stud dog is what type of puppies he has produced, and with what bloodlines, and whether or not he possesses the bloodlines and attributes considered characteristic of the best in your breed.

If you go out to buy a stud dog, obviously he will not be a puppy, but rather a fully mature and proven male with as many of the best attributes as possible. True, he will be an expensive investment, but if you choose and make his selection with care and forethought, he may well prove to be one of the best investments you have ever made.

Of course, the most exciting of all is when a young male you have decided to keep from one of your litters, due to his tremendous show potential, turns out to be a stud dog such as we have described. In this case he should be managed with care, for he is a valuable property that can contribute inestimably to this breed as a whole and to your own kennel specifically.

Although not standing at her best, one cannot miss the quality of Ch. Morning Star's Little Pomeroy as she wins a Group at Bucks County in 1949, Harry Clasen handling.

This is Ch. Zodiac's Special Beau, owned by Robert L. Breum, a show dog and sire of true excellence in the breed.

Do not permit your stud dog to be used until he is about a year old, and even then he should be bred to a mature, proven matron accustomed to breeding who will make his first experience pleasant and easy. A young dog can be put off forever by a maiden bitch who fights and resists his advances. Never allow this to happen. Always start a stud dog out with a bitch who is mature, has been bred previously, and is of even temperament. The first breeding should be performed in quiet surroundings with only you and one other person to hold the bitch. Do not make it a circus, as the experience will determine the dog's outlook about future stud work. If he does not enjoy the first experience or associates it with any unpleasantness, you may well have a problem in the future.

Your young stud must permit help with the breeding, as later there will be bitches who will not be cooperative. If right from the beginning you are there helping him and praising him, whether or not your assistance is actually needed, he will expect and accept this as a matter of course when a difficult bitch comes along.

Things to have handy before introducing your dog and the bitch are K-Y jelly (the only lubricant which should be used) and a length of gauze with which to muzzle the bitch should it be necessary to keep her from biting you or the dog. Some bitches put up a fight; others are calm. It is best to be prepared.

At the time of the breeding, the stud fee comes due, and it is expected that it will be paid promptly. Normally a return service is offered in case the bitch misses or fails to produce one live puppy. Conditions of the service are what the stud dog's owner makes them, and there are no standard rules covering this. The stud fee is paid for the act, not the result. If the bitch fails to conceive, it is customary for the owner to offer a free return service; but this is a courtesy and not to be considered a right, particularly in the case of a proven stud who is siring consistently and whose fault the failure obviously is *not*. Stud dog owners are always anxious to see their clients get good value and to have in the ring winning young stock by their dog; therefore, very few refuse to mate the second time. It is wise, however, for both parties to have the terms of the transaction clearly understood at the time of the breeding.

If the return service has been provided and the bitch has missed a second time, that is considered to be the end of the matter and the owner would be expected to pay a further fee if it is felt that the bitch should be given a third chance with the stud dog. The management of a stud dog and his visiting bitches is quite a task, and a stud fee has usually been well earned when one service has been achieved, let alone by repeated visits from the same bitch.

The accepted litter is one live puppy. It is wise to have printed a breeding certificate which the owner of the stud dog and the owner of the bitch both sign. This should list in detail the conditions of the breeding as well as the dates of the mating.

Upon occasion, arrangements other than a stud fee in cash are made for a breeding, such as the owner of the stud taking a pick-of-the-litter puppy in lieu of money. This should be clearly specified on the breeding certificate along with the terms of the age at which the stud's owner will select the puppy, whether it is to be a specific sex, or whether it is to be the pick of the entire litter.

The price of a stud fee varies according to circumstances. Usually, to prove a young stud dog, his owner will allow the first breeding to be quite inexpensive. Then, once a bitch has become pregnant by him, he becomes a "proven stud" and the fee rises accordingly for bitches that follow. The sire of championship quality puppies will bring a stud fee of at least the purchase price of one show puppy as the accepted "rule-of-thumb." Until at least one champion by your stud dog has finished, the fee will remain equal to the price of one pet puppy. When his list of champions starts to grow, so does the amount of the stud fee. For a top-producing sire of champions, the stud fee will rise accordingly.

Almost invariably it is the bitch who comes to the stud dog for the breeding. Immediately upon having selected the stud dog you wish to use, discuss the possibility with the owner of that dog. It is the stud dog owner's prerogative to refuse to breed any bitch deemed unsuitable for this dog. Stud fee and method of payment should be stated at this time and a decision reached on whether it is to be a full cash transaction at the time of the mating or a pick-of-the-litter puppy, usually at eight weeks of age.

If the owner of the stud dog must travel to an airport to meet the bitch and ship her for the flight home, an additional charge will be made for time, tolls, and gasoline based on the stud owner's proximity to the airport. The stud fee includes board for the day on the bitch's arrival through two days for breeding, with a day in between. If it is necessary that the bitch remain longer, it is very likely that additional board will be charged at the normal per-day rate for the breed.

Be sure to advise the stud's owner as soon as you know that your bitch is in season so that the stud dog will be available. This is especially important because if he is a dog being shown, he and his owner may be unavailable, owing to the dog's absence from home.

As the owner of a stud dog being offered to the public, it is essential that you have proper facilities for the care of visiting bitches. Nothing can be worse than a bitch being insecurely housed and slipping out to become lost or bred by the wrong dog. If you are taking people's valued bitches into your kennel or home, it is imperative that you provide them with comfortable, secure housing and good care while they are your responsibility.

There is no dog more valuable than the proven sire of champions, Group winners, and Best in Show dogs. Once you have such an animal, guard his reputation well and do *not* permit him to be bred to just any bitch that comes along. It takes two to make the puppies; even the most dominant stud cannot do it all himself, so never permit him to breed a bitch you consider unworthy. Remember that when the puppies arrive, it will be your stud dog who will be blamed for any lack of quality, while the bitch's shortcomings will be quickly and conveniently overlooked.

Going into the actual management of the mating is a bit superfluous here. If you have had previous experience in breeding a dog and bitch, you will know how the mating is done. If you do not have such experience, you should not attempt to follow directions given in a book but should have a veterinarian, breeder friend, or handler there to help you with the first few times. You do not just turn the dog and bitch loose together and await developments, as too many things can go wrong and you may altogether miss getting the bitch bred. Someone should hold the dog and the bitch (one person each) until the "tie" is made and these two people should stay with them during the entire act.

If you get a complete tie, probably only the one mating is absolutely necessary. However, especially with a maiden bitch or one that has come a long distance for this breeding, a follow-up with a second breeding is preferred, leaving one day in between the two matings. In this way there will be little or no chance of the bitch missing.

Once the tie has been completed and the dogs release, be certain that the male's penis goes completely back within its sheath. He should be allowed a drink of water and a short walk, and then he should be put into his crate or somewhere alone where he can settle down. Do not allow him to be with other dogs for a while as they will notice the odor of the bitch on him, and, particularly with other males present, he may become involved in a fight.

PREGNANCY, WHELPING, AND THE LITTER

Once the bitch has been bred and is back at home, remember to keep an ever watchful eye that no other males get to her until at least the twenty-second day of her season has passed. Until then, it will still be possible for an unwanted breeding to take place, which at this point would be catastrophic. Remember that she actually can have two separate litters by two different dogs, so take care.

In other ways, she should be treated normally. Controlled exercise is good and necessary for the bitch throughout her pregnancy, tapering it off to just several short walks daily, preferably on lead, as she reaches about her seventh week. As her time grows close, be careful about her jumping or playing too roughly.

The theory that a bitch should be overstuffed with food when pregnant is a poor one. A fat bitch is never an easy whelper, so the overfeeding you consider good for her may well turn out to be a hindrance later on. During the first few weeks of pregnancy, your bitch should be fed her normal diet. At four to five weeks along, calcium should be added to her food. At seven weeks her food may be increased if she seems to crave more than she is getting, and a meal of canned milk (mixed with an equal amount of water) should be introduced. If she is fed just once a day, add another meal rather than overload her with too much at one time. If twice a day is her schedule, then a bit more food can be added to each feeding.

A week before the pups are due, your bitch should be introduced to her whelping box so that she will be accustomed to it and feel at home there when the puppies arrive. She should be encouraged to sleep there but permitted to come and go as she wishes. The box should be roomy enough for her to lie down and stretch out in but not too large, lest the pups have more room than is needed in which to roam and possibly get chilled by going too far away from their mother. Be sure that the box has a "pig rail"; this will prevent the puppies from being crushed against the sides. The room in which the box is placed, either in your home or in the kennel, should be kept at about 70 degrees Fahrenheit. In winter it may be necessary to have an infrared lamp over the whelping box, in which case be careful not to place it too low or close to the puppies.

Newspapers will become a very important commodity, so start collecting them well in advance to have a big pile handy for the whelping box. With a litter of puppies, one never seems to have papers enough, so the higher pile to start with, the better off you will be. Other necessities for whelping time are clean, soft turkish towels, scissors, and a bottle of alcohol.

You will know that her time is very near when your bitch becomes restless, wandering in and out of her box and out of the room. She may refuse food, and at that point her temperature will start to drop. She will dig at and tear up the newspapers in her box, shiver, and generally look uncomfortable. Only you should be with your bitch at this time. She does not need spectators; and several people hanging over her, even though they may be family members whom she knows, may upset her to the point where she may harm the puppies. You should remain nearby, quietly watching, not fussing or hovering; speak calmly and frequently to her to instill confidence. Eventually she will settle down in her box and begin panting; contractions will follow. Soon thereafter a puppy will start to emerge, sliding out with the contractions. The mother immediately should open the sac, sever the cord with her teeth, and then clean up the puppy. She will also eat the placenta, which you should permit. Once the puppy is cleaned, it should be placed next to the bitch unless she is showing signs of having the next one immediately. Almost at once the puppy will start looking for a nipple on which to nurse, and you should ascertain that it is able to latch on successfully.

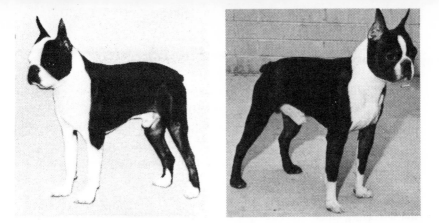

Left: The very famous Ch. Toby Junior II, who died in February 1982, was one of Harry Clasen's greatest. By Clasen's Mastar ex Bee Bee X, Toby was in the Top Ten Bostons while being shown and became the sire of 21 champions. Photo courtesy of Mrs. Clasen, Mechanicville, New York. *Right:* Ch. B.B.'s Dudes Little Hobo is the sire of many champion sons and daughters. He is by Ch. Eanes Dude The Little Rebel ex Ch. Toy Town's High Stepping Lana, was bred by Elaine Newbecker, and is owned by Neva Stewart, Fairfax, Virginia.

"They're mine" is what Dancing's Lil Jewel Pandora's expression says as she guards champions-to-be Regal Legacy Golden Gladiator and Regal Legacy's Night Raider Lust. These pups were sired by Am. and Can. Ch. Simms Hi-hope Mr. Hobo. Bred and owned by Jose F. Negron and Anthony A. Antolics, Annandale, Virginia.

If the puppy is a breech (*i.e.*, born feet first), you must watch carefully for it to be completely delivered as quickly as possible and for the sac to be removed quickly so that the puppy does not drown. Sometimes even a normally positioned birth will seem extremely slow in coming. Should this occur, you might take a clean towel, and as the bitch contracts, pull the puppy out, doing so gently and with utmost care. If, once the puppy is delivered, it shows little signs of life, take a rough turkish towel and massage the puppy's chest by rubbing quite briskly back and forth. Continue this for about fifteen minutes, and be sure that the mouth is free of liquid. It may be necessary to try mouth-to-mouth breathing, which is done by pressing the puppy's jaws open and, using a finger, depressing the tongue which may be stuck to the roof of the mouth. Then place your mouth against the puppy's and blow hard down the puppy's throat. Rub the puppy's chest with the towel again and try artificial respiration, pressing the sides of the chest together slowly and rhythmically—in and out, in and out. Keep trying one method or the other for at least twenty minutes before giving up. You may be rewarded with a live puppy who otherwise would not have made it.

If you are successful in bringing the puppy around, do not immediately put it back with the mother as it should be kept extra warm. Put it in a cardboard box on an electric heating pad or, if it is the time of year when your heat is running, near a radiator or near the fireplace or stove. As soon as the rest of the litter has been born, it then can join the others.

An hour or more may elapse between puppies, which is fine so long as the bitch seems comfortable and is neither straining nor contracting. She should not be permitted to remain unassisted for more than an hour if she does continue to contract. This is when you should get her to your veterinarian, whom you should already have alerted to the possibility of a problem existing. He should examine her and perhaps give her a shot of Pituitrin. In some cases the veterinarian may find that a Caesarean section is necessary due to a puppy being lodged in a manner making normal delivery impossible. Sometimes this is caused by an abnormally large puppy, or it may just be that the puppy is simply turned in the wrong position. If the bitch does require a Caesarean section, the puppies already born must be kept warm in their cardboard box with a heating pad under the box.

Once the section is done, get the bitch and the puppies home. Do not attempt to put the puppies in with the bitch until she has regained consciousness, as she may unknowingly hurt them. But do get them back to her as soon as possible for them to start nursing.

Should the mother lack milk at this time, the puppies must be fed by hand, kept very warm, and held onto the mother's teats several times a day in order to stimulate and encourage the secretion of milk, which should start shortly.

Assuming that there has been no problem and that the bitch has whelped naturally, you should insist that she go out to exercise, staying just long enough to make herself comfortable. She can be offered a bowl of milk and a biscuit, but then she should settle down with her family. Freshen the whelping box for her with fresh newspapers while she is taking this respite so that she and the puppies will have a clean bed.

Unless some problem arises, there is little you must do for the puppies until they become three to four weeks old. Keep the box clean and supplied with fresh newspapers the first few days, but then turkish towels should be tacked down to the bottom of the box so that the puppies will have traction as they move about.

If the bitch has difficulties with her milk supply, or if you should be so unfortunate as to lose her, then you must be prepared to either hand-feed or tube-feed the puppies if they are to survive. Tube-feeding is so much faster and easier. If the bitch is available, it is best that she continues to clean and care for the puppies in the normal manner, excepting for the food supplements you will provide. If it is impossible for her to do this, then after every feeding you must gently rub each puppy's abdomen with wet cotton to make it urinate, and the rectum should be gently rubbed to open the bowels.

Newborn puppies must be fed every three to four hours around the clock. The puppies must be kept warm during this time. Have your veterinarian teach you how to tube-feed. You will find that it is really quite simple.

After a normal whelping, the bitch will require additional food to enable her to produce sufficient milk. In addition to being fed twice daily, she should be given some canned milk several times each day.

When the puppies are two weeks old, their nails should be clipped, as they are needle sharp at this age and can hurt or damage the mother's teats and stomach as the pups hold on to nurse.

Between three and four weeks of age, the puppies should begin to be weaned. Scraped beef (prepared by scraping it off slices of beef with a spoon so that none of the gristle is included) may be offered in very small quantities a couple of times daily for the first few days. Then by the third day you can mix puppy chow with warm water as directed on the package, offering it four times daily. By now the mother should be kept away from the puppies and out of the box for several hours at a time so that when they have reached five weeks of age she is left in with them only overnight. By the time the puppies are six weeks old, they should be entirely weaned and receiving only occasional visits from their mother.

Most veterinarians recommend a temporary DHL (distemper, hepatitis, leptospirosis) shot when the puppies are six weeks of age. This remains effective for about two weeks. Then at eight weeks of age, the puppies should receive the series of permanent shots for DHL protection. It is also a good idea to discuss with your vet the advisability of having your puppies inoculated against the dreaded parvovirus at the same time. Each time the pups go to the vet for shots, you should bring stool samples so that they can be examined for worms. Worms go through various stages of development and may be present in a stool sample even though the sample does not test positive in every checkup. So do not neglect to keep careful watch on this.

The puppies should be fed four times daily until they are three months old. Then you can cut back to three feedings daily. By the time the puppies are six months of age, two meals daily are sufficient. Some people feed their dogs twice daily throughout their lifetime; others go to one meal daily when the puppy becomes one year of age.

The ideal age for puppies to go to their new homes is between eight and twelve weeks, although some puppies successfully adjust to a new home when they are six weeks old. Be sure that they go

Ch. Schubo's Gleamin' Golden Girl, by Ch. Georgia Girl's Chappie ex Ch. Schubo's Flashin' Gold Dust, homebred and owned by Wes and Karen Schultz, Schubo Bostons, Amarillo, Texas.

to their new owners accompanied by a description of the diet you've been feeding them and a schedule of the shots they have already received and those they still need. These should be included with the registration application and a copy of the pedigree.

Ch. Chappie's Regards, by Ch. Griffing's Little Chappie ex Ch. Dundee Bonnie Regards, winning an all-breed Best in Show under Marie Meyers. Owned by John T. Robinson. Photo from the collection of Leonard L. Myers, Denver, Colorado.

Chapter 14

Traveling with Your Boston Terrier

When you travel with your dog, to shows or on vacation or wherever, remember that everyone does not share your enthusiasm or love for dogs and that those who do not, strange creatures though they seem to us, have their rights too. These rights, on which you should not encroach, include not being disturbed, annoyed, or made uncomfortable by the presence and behavior of other people's pets. Your dog should be kept on lead in public places and should recognize and promptly obey the commands "Down," "Come," "Sit," and "Stay."

Take along his crate if you are going any distance with your dog. And keep him in it when riding in the car. A crated dog has a far better chance of escaping injury than one riding loose in the car, should an accident occur or an emergency arise. If you do permit your dog to ride loose, never allow him to hang out a window, ears blowing in the breeze. An injury to his eyes could occur in this manner. He could also become overly excited by something he sees and jump out, or he could lose his balance and fall out.

Never, ever, under any circumstances, should a dog be permitted to ride loose in the back of a pick-up truck. Some people do transport dogs in this manner, which is cruel and shocking. How easily such a dog can be thrown out of the truck by sudden jolts or an impact! Doubtless many dogs have jumped out at the sight of something exciting along the way. Some unthinking individuals tie the dog, probably not realizing that were he to jump under those circumstances, his neck would be broken, he could be dragged alongside the vehicle, or he could be hit by another vehicle. If for any reason you are taking your dog in an open-back truck, please have sufficient regard for that dog to at least provide a crate for him; and then remember that, in or out of a crate, a dog riding under the direct rays of the sun in hot weather can suffer and have his life endangered by the heat.

If you are staying at a hotel or motel with your dog, exercise him somewhere other than in the flower beds and parking lot of the property. People walking to and from their cars really are not thrilled at "stepping in something" left by your dog. Should an accident occur, pick it up with a tissue or paper towel and deposit it in a proper receptacle; do not just walk off leaving it to remain there. Usually there are grassy areas on the sides of and behind motels where dogs can be exercised. Use them rather than the more conspicuous, usually carefully tended, front areas or those close to the rooms. If you are becoming a dog show enthusiast, you will eventually need an exercise pen to take with you to the show. Exercise pens are ideal to use when staying at motels, too, as they permit you to limit the dog's roaming space and to pick up after him more easily.

Never leave your dog unattended in the room of a motel unless you are absolutely, positively certain that he will stay there quietly and not damage or destroy anything. You do not want a long list of complaints from irate guests, caused by the annoying barking or whining of a lonesome dog in strange surroundings or an over-zealous watch dog barking furiously each time a footstep passes the door or he hears a sound from an adjoining room. And you certainly do not want to return to torn curtains or bedspreads, soiled rugs, or other embarrassing evidence of the fact that your dog is not really house-reliable after all.

If yours is a dog accustomed to traveling with you and you are positive that his behavior will be acceptable when left alone, that is fine. But if the slightest uncertainty exists, the wise course is to

Ch. Chahary Une Baiser Moi Kismet, handled by breeder-owner Mrs. Ira Smoluchowski, is a daughter of Ch. Unique's Royalty Kid ex Chahary Beau Kay Zizani. Completed title at age 11 months at Westminster K.C. A champion producer as well.

leave him in the car while you go to dinner or elsewhere; then bring him into the room when you are ready to retire for the night.

When you travel with a dog, it is often simpler to take along from home the food and water he will need rather than to buy food and look for water while you travel. In this way he will have the rations to which he is accustomed and which you know agree with him, and there will be no fear of problems due to different drinking water. Feeding on the road is quite easy now, at least for short trips, with all the splendid dry prepared foods and high-quality canned meats available. A variety of lightweight, refillable water containers can be bought at many types of stores.

Always be careful to leave sufficient openings to ventilate your car when the dog will be alone in it. Remember that during the summer, the rays of the sun can make an inferno of a closed car

This lovely bitch, Ch. What's Up Tiger Lily, owned by Judy Griffith and Maxine Uzoff, pictured taking Best of Breed and Group 3rd under famous breeder-judge, the late Vince Perry.

within only a few minutes, so leave enough window space open to provide air circulation. Again, if your dog is in a crate, this can be done quite safely. The fact that you have left the car in a shady spot is not always a guarantee that you will find conditions the same when you return. Don't forget that the position of the sun changes in a matter of minutes, and the car you left nicely shaded half an hour ago can be getting full sunlight far more quickly than you may realize. So, if you leave a dog in the car, make sure there is sufficient ventilation and check back frequently to ascertain that all is well.

If you are going to another country, you will need a health certificate from your veterinarian for each dog you are taking with you, certifying that each has had rabies shots within the required time preceding your visit.

Index

285

Index of People

Edmiston, Sadie, 54
Edwards, Mrs. H.E., 182
Ely, Mr. & Mrs. W.C., 25
Enwright, Jackie, 197
Enwright, Thomas L., 53, 106, 119, 138, 154, 197, 262
Erickson, Pat, 50, 73
Erwin, C.J., 73
Faigel, Joe, 3, 22, 24
Feder, Julius C., 18
Ferguson, Marie, 67
Fitzgerald, Claude J., 25
Fitzgerald, Mr. & Mrs. Claude, 29
Flowers, Stan, 68, 69
Ford, Freeman, 12, 18
Fottrell, Helen, 67
Foy, Marcia A., 8
Fraser, Lois, 51, 52, 53, 106
Fritz, Helen, 258
Galor, Cindy, 110, 68-69
Galor, Ed, 68-69, 110
Glaser, Joe, 26, 184, 258
Gleason, Florence, 122
Godsol, Mrs. Beatrice, 29, 203
Googe, A.L., 15
Goss, Terry, 126, 142, 158, 170-172, 211
Grant, Mrs. Parker, 114
Griffing, Anne/Bob, 26, 203
Griffith, Judy, 91, 118, 127, 151, 284
Gulledge, Yvette C., 83, 84-85, 265
Hall, Forest, 54
Harig, Mr. & Mrs. John, 86
Harris, Mary, 96
Haupt, William, 246
Hayhurst, Mrs., 167
Heffron, Miss Marie, 45
Heit, Mrs. Eleanor, 122
Heit, Murray A., 122, 162-163
Hirlinger, Marilyn, 73
Hite, Dr. K. Eileen, 23, 29
Hodge, Mrs. Lomer (Dorene), 122, 126, 167, 169-170, 173
Hodgins, Mrs. G.A., 126
Hoffman, Ellen, 74
Hoggman, Ellen, 139
Hooper, Robert C., 12
Huddleston, Arthur/Lillian, 27, 79-82, 174, 197, 232, 261
Hunter, Wilma, 114
Jeffords, Mrs. Walter (Kay), 55-56, 57, 65, 74, 106, 107, 111, 131, 147, 150, 154, 194
Johnson, Helen, 66
Johnson, Johnny/Patricia, 93

Kay, Jane, 79, 114
Kelly, John A., 18, 158
Kelly, Kathleen, 174
Kelly, Marby, 158
Kendall, Dr. W. G., 18, 20
Kendrick, William, 122
Kenwell, H.W., 25
Kibler, Ray A., 59, 259
Kibler, Roy S., 174
Klein, Ed, 68
Klinckhardt, Emil, 68, 150
Koenigsberg, Mrs. Elsie, 182
Krebs, Larry, 33
Kubach, William F., 18, 20
Kurtz, Mrs. J.R., 25
Lamb, Miss Ina, 174
Land, Eric J.C., 26
Lee, Alvin M., Jr., 94
Lehr, Mina, 174
Lieberg, Ruth, 174
Lowes, Bob/Dianne, 73, 122, 126, 127, 164, 165-168, 250
Lowes, Lorna, 139
Lucas, Fred/Mary, 16, 25, 26
Lunan, John C., 21
Lynch, Matthias, 16
McCushing, Dr. George J. B., 18, 25
McFarland, Lyda, 252
McGlone, Mrs. Madelaine, 25
McMahon, Mary, 102
Marchise, Gene, 40
Martell, Julius/Willie Mae, 61, 63-64, 67, 107, 110, 130, 135, 151
Marvel, Robert, 90, 253
Meyers, Marie, 280
Middleton, John A., 27
Milham, Bob/Karen, 36, 38, 99, 119
Miller, Lee, 73
Montecalvo, Frank, 203
Moore, Mrs. Ralph C., 56
Munroe, Mr. & Mrs. Les H., 162
Munson, Byron/Doris, 27, 40-43, 102, 119
Myers, Leonard L., 13, 19, 41, 56-59, 107, 118, 155, 179, 203, 259, 280
Negron, Jose F., 70-71, 111, 134, 135, 139, 142, 143, 150, 151, 154, 159, 232, 275
Neigenfind, Mrs. Billie, 53, 54
Newbecker, Elaine, 245, 275
Niebauer, Joseph, 64, 66-68, 110
Niebauer, Mary Alice, 64, 66-68, 110, 174, 219
O'Brien, William, 12

287

This Book belongs to the
Sparsholt College Library.